"After shooting a daily television show outdoors for many years in the San Diego area, I thought we had just about found all the great locations. To my surprise, the authors have come up with many beautiful spots even we didn't know about. The book is a valuable tool for anyone in my business."

——Dave Hood, Host/Producer
PM Magazine, KFMB–TV

"Families, couples and singles will enjoy exploring the coastal and inland natural spaces that Moore and Hewitt describe in *Walking San Diego*. Teachers will find it a good resource for field trips. The history and natural history descriptions are a plus for people who have a curiosity about the place they are visiting. Where can you find a more thorough guide to the "little nature trips around San Diego?" There aren't any others."

——Skip Ruland, President
Wilderness Center of San Diego

"Whether you want solitude, inspiration, entertainment, education, or just good, scenic exercise, *Walking San Diego* will be a treasure guide to countless hours of fascinating pleasure and discovery."

——Philip R. Pryde, Editor
San Diego: An Introduction to the
Region

"As a long-time resident of San Diego, I have often looked for a complete guide to the local nature trails. I am glad someone has finally put together such a book, and am looking forward to exploring parts of our county that I have never seen."

——Rolf Benirschke, former placekicker
The San Diego Chargers

"For 'insider' trips, tips and truth (walking times, distances, attractions, and even weather) about San Diego, this is a winner for walkers. It'll make you Balboa for a day, or a week!"

——Brad Ketchum, Jr., editor
The Walking Magazine

WALKING
SAN DIEGO

Where to Go to Get Away
From It All & What to Do
When You Get There

Lonnie Burstein Hewitt
& Barbara Coffin Moore

THE MOUNTAINEERS

The Mountaineers: Organized 1906 "... to explore, study, preserve, and enjoy the natural beauty of the Northwest."

3 2
5 4 3 2

Published by The Mountaineers
1011 S.W. Klickitat Way, Suite 107, Seattle, Washington 98134

Published simultaneously in Canada by Douglas & McIntyre, Ltd., 1615 Venables Street, Vancouver, B.C. V5L 2H1

Published simultaneously in Britain by Cordee, 3a DeMontfort St., Leicester, England LE1 7HD

Manufactured in the United States of America

Edited by Jim Jensen
Maps by Jo P. Griffith
All photographs by Susan Green unless otherwise credited
Cover photographs:
    Top—bush monkey flower (photo courtesy Torrey Pines State Reserve).
    Top right—mariposa lily with yellow spider; center right—at San Elijo Lagoon;
        bottom right—barrel cactus (photos by Barbara Moore).
    Left—birdwatcher in Los Peñasquitos Canyon Preserve (photo © Bill Evarts, 1989).
    Frontispiece: Tidepools at Cabrillo National Monument. Page 23: Bird man at the beach.
    Page 82: Lake Jennings. Page 83: Waterfall at Felicita Park (photo by Barbara Moore).
    Page 178: Solitary beach walker. Page 223: Bush poppy.
Cover design by Betty Watson
Book design by Constance Bollen

Library of Congress Cataloging in Publication Data

Hewitt, Lonnie Burstein, 1942-
    Walking San Diego.

    Includes bibliographical references.
    1. Walking—California—San Diego—Guide books.
2. Hiking—California—San Diego—Guide books.
3. San Diego (Calif.)—Description—Guide books.
I. Moore, Barbara Coffin.   II. Title.
GV199.42.C22S264   1989   917.94'985   89-13053
ISBN 0-89886-221-3

To our fathers, who would have enjoyed these walks

◆ ACKNOWLEDGMENTS ◆

Walking San Diego has been a big part of our lives for over a year, and many people have helped to make it possible. We'd like to thank the park rangers, city and county officials, naturalists, and historians who gave us hours of their time and interest, with special thanks to the very knowledgeable Hank Nicol, for reviewing the entire manuscript. Thanks to our photographer, Susan R. Green; our mapmaker, Jo P. Griffith; and our artists, Kathryn Watson and David Stump; for their invaluable contributions. Thanks to our families, friends, students, and associates for putting up with our monomania, to all the walkers, cyclists, and horseback riders who answered our questions on the trails, and to Maurice Hewitt, husband and friend, for help and encouragement beyond the call of duty.

A NOTE ON SAFETY

Safety is an important concern in all outdoor activities. No guidebook can alert you to every hazard or anticipate the limitations of every reader, so the descriptions in this book are not representations that a particular trip is safe for your party. When you take a trip, you assume responsibility for your own safety. Some of the trips described in this book may require you to do no more than look both ways before crossing the street; on others, more attention to safety may be required due to terrain, traffic, weather, the capabilities of your party, or other factors. Keeping informed on current conditions and exercising common sense are the keys to a safe, enjoyable outing.

The Publisher

◆ CONTENTS ◆

The authors at work: Barbara Moore (left) and Lonnie Hewitt

◆ AUTHORS' NOTE ◆

Once a small town with a military air, San Diego is today the fastest growing area in California. Over 32 million people visit here every year, and many of them never leave. The countywide population is 2.3 million, with another half million expected by the turn of the century. San Diego is now the seventh largest city in the country.

Rapid growth has brought new problems. Air and water quality are not what they used to be, and sometimes freeway traffic is uncomfortably like L.A.'s. Our hillsides have been stripped, flattened, and covered with buildings; the wide open spaces have virtually disappeared.

But there are still a surprising number of lovely and little-known places where you can find a quiet spot for a hike, a picnic, or just a breath of traffic-free air—even on a summer Sunday.

Here are some of our favorites, enough for months of outings. We've tried to point you in the best directions, and tell you about the plants, birds, and animals you'll see along the way. We've included some local history, a few outdoor do-it-yourself projects, and as many odd and interesting facts as we could fit in, and still keep the whole thing easy to read and carry. You can count on doing some walking, but nothing strenuous; most of our walks are about two hours long, suitable for all ages, and less than an hour's drive from downtown.

We've had such fun collecting material for *Walking San Diego* we can't wait to share it. Once you start exploring the trails for yourself, we think you'll see what we mean. These are places to return to again and again, with every season a little bit different and every visit a new adventure.

If you have any additions or suggestions, please let us hear from you. Meanwhile, happy trails!

Lonnie & Barbara

Del Mar, California
April 1989

Sunday in the park with Dad

◆ A WORD TO THE WALKER ◆

Some of the walks in this book are strolls; some are more like hikes. All of them can be done by anyone in reasonably good physical condition, without any special hiking skills or shoes. In fact, one of us often hits the trail, weather permitting, in rubber thongs.

But we don't recommend such eccentricity. Cushioned running or walking shoes are best—comfortable ones with a decent tread, so you don't lose your grip on the road. A walking stick can be useful too, especially on hills; it's always nice to have an extra leg to stand on.

Walking is great exercise, and a brisk walk uphill can be just as good a cardiovascular workout as jogging, without the shin splints and back strain. But walking briskly often means you miss a lot of what we're walking for—the sights and sounds of our natural environment.

We usually figure on a 20- to 30-minute flat mile, taking plenty of time to smell the flowers. If you want more action, try pumping your arms as you walk, like a sprinter. Breathe deeply. Smile! It's not just the exercise, but the sense of well-being that comes from an hour or two spent on your own two feet in the fresh, fume-less air that really does your heart good!

Though we think all our trails are safe and not terribly strenuous, a normal amount of caution is advised. Stay on the marked trails; shortcuts can be dangerous to you and the wildlife you trample. Watch your step on rocky paths, and on wet ones, where things can get slippery. It goes without saying that children especially should be watched carefully, particularly around cliffs and canyons.

Times being what they are, it's not such a great idea to go walking alone. If you don't have a regular walking companion, ask around, advertise in your local paper, or join a group. There's safety in numbers, and it's nice to share your discoveries.

The Natural History Museum's Canyoneers, the Audubon Society, adult schools, and other organizations frequently offer guided walks. Check the outdoor activities or weekend section of your newspaper.

WHAT TO WEAR, WHAT TO CARRY

Next to walking or running shoes, sun visors are our most valued piece of attire. Even if you're caught in the rain, a visor can help keep your glasses dry. On rougher trails, long pants protect you from the shrubbery and any leg-loving insects.

Here's a suggestion of what you might want to bring along, remembering, of course, that he (or she) travels best who travels light. A small day pack should carry everything you could possibly want or need and still leave your hands free for your walking stick, binoculars, camera, or notepad.

- Sunscreen, especially in summer
- Binoculars for viewing birds and distant flowers
- Notepad and pen for notes and plant sketches
- Sweater or windbreaker for unexpected weather changes
- Camera
- Bandaids and antiseptic, just in case
- Snacks or picnic lunch
- A small water bottle (Hot tip: Put your water bottle in the freezer the night before; don't fill it too full or it will crack. This gives you ice water for hot-day hikes.)

Actually, we keep a few essentials in the back of the car: an extra pair of socks and sneakers, a jacket, a walking stick, and a sun visor. That way, we're always ready!

WEATHER OR NOT

San Diego's reputation as a place of year-round perfect weather is a little misleading. Generally speaking, we don't have four seasons, but two: winter/wet and summer/dry. But some years are wetter than others, with destructive storms flooding beach towns and valleys, and some are bone-dry, draining our reservoirs.

Depending on how much rain there's been, spring wildflowers may come out in January or April. September and October are often the hottest months, and summer may be no summer at all, especially along the coast, which can be damp, cool, and foggy, while inland temperatures soar into the 90s. Winter can bring snow to the mountains, but anywhere else, it's highly unlikely. Any time of year, mornings and evenings can be chilly; 30-degree swings in temperature are not unusual.

What all this means is—be prepared. The layered look is always appropriate: a sweater on top of a long-sleeved shirt on top of a short-sleeved one. Then you're covered—or uncovered—no matter what weather comes up.

Unhappily, smog has made its way to San Diego, and it can be a real irritant to some walkers, causing breathing difficulty, stinging eyes, and other allergic symptoms. In early fall, the hot desert winds called Santa

Anas blow pollutants out to sea, but as the winds weaken, a southward drift takes over, and we end up with a swirl of smog from L.A. If you're sensitive, you'll feel it long before smog alerts are announced. For a report on the latest conditions, call Air Pollution Control at 565-6626.

Since weather can vary greatly from day to day and place to place, you might want to check with the weather bureau before deciding which way to go. You can get a comprehensive, countywide forecast anytime by calling 289-1212.

TRAIL DO'S AND DON'TS

Don't take living souvenirs. Nearly all our sites are protected and none of them could stand the strain of every visitor picking just one little wildflower.

Don't take our mention of Indian usages of plants for an endorsement. Don't taste anything you're not absolutely sure you know.

Los Peñasquitos Canyon

Gopher snake (top left) and rattlesnake. Drawings by David Stump

A WORD ABOUT SNAKES

Of all the county's 33 species of snakes, rattlesnakes are the only ones to be concerned about. Easily recognized by their triangular heads and the warning rattles at the end of their tails, they're wonderful to watch—from a safe distance.

Members of the pit viper family, rattlesnakes have heat-sensitive pits on each side of their heads, which help them sense the presence of mice or gophers in the dark and human walkers in the daytime. Like us, they want to avoid confrontation; the greatest danger is stepping on a sleeping snake. Abruptly awakened, it's likely to strike first and rattle a warning later.

All snakes are cold-blooded animals that need to be warm to digest their food. A cold snake can actually die of indigestion. That's why they're most frequently seen in spring, stretched out in the sun after a meal. Snakes in Southern California don't hibernate in winter, as they do in colder climates; whenever it's warm enough, they do their hunting and digesting at night.

If you should see a rattlesnake, just back away slowly; it will probably do the same. Don't yell, wave your arms, or try to frighten the snake; you'll only confuse it.

If worst comes to worst, and you do get bitten, don't panic. Tie a constrictive band 4 to 6 inches above the bite; don't tie it too tightly, and don't apply ice. If you're out in the middle of nowhere, start walking slowly back toward civilization; the best remedy for snakebite is your car key. Head for the nearest hospital; antivenin is available throughout the county. For more information, call the Poison Center at 543-6000.

Don't forget: "Leaves of three, let it be." Learn how to recognize poison oak in all seasons, and keep out of it (see Appendix A).

Don't tease any animal, or pet anything that doesn't belong to you. Wildlife should be admired, and treated with respect. Keep an eye out for rattlesnakes, especially in springtime.

Last but not least—do we have to say it?—don't litter. Trashing our wild spaces will leave us nothing worth walking to. As city trash can signs once said: Every Litter Bit Hurts.

Lest we start sounding too negative, here are some do's:

Do take time to look for animal tracks, listen to a bird's song, or admire a tiny flower. That's what *Walking San Diego* is all about. Just giving the area a once-over glance, you might miss such camouflaged creatures as the horned lizard, one of our favorites.

Do feel free to do half a walk, or less, or more, as the spirit moves you. Scribble in the book, add your personal notes, make it your own.

And please, do enjoy yourself. We mean these walks to be fun!

A Word About... The Book

Walking San Diego is as user friendly as we could make it. Dip in wherever you like, depending on where you want to go; you don't have to read it in order.

The "TB numbers" at each location refer to the Thomas Brothers Street Guide and Directory, which many San Diegans swear by. The page number is followed by map coordinates.

Kumeyaay mother and child. Photo courtesy Mountain Empire Historical Society

◆ SAN DIEGO, THEN AND NOW ◆

In the days when dinosaurs still roamed the earth, San Diego was a series of volcanic islands, mostly under water. As the seas receded, the islands rose, becoming mountains. Over millions of years, they were worn down by the elements into masses of sediment that formed a great coastal plain.

About 22 million years ago, this coastal plain was jolted by seismic activity and resurfaced as new mountain ranges extending from Los Angeles into Baja California.

San Diego was probably a more wooded place, and warmer, when the earliest human inhabitants arrived about 10,000 years ago. They were stone-age hunters, following herds of large and edible animals—mammoths, bison, and saber-toothed tigers—across the bridge of land from Asia to Alaska, and down the coast. Apart from some crude stone tools, they left few relics of their existence. As one of their key sites was along what the Spanish called the San Dieguito River, they are sometimes referred to as the San Dieguito culture.

Next on the scene were the La Jollans, who settled near coastal lagoons where fish and shellfish were plentiful. Though archaeologists once assumed they had succeeded the San Dieguito people, more recent discoveries show they may have lived here at about the same time. Whether they were part of the same culture or another one is still open to question.

The last group of "Indians"—Columbus' misnomer that blankets all the original inhabitants of the New World—came westward from the Colorado River Valley about 1200 years ago. They knew how to use bows and arrows, make pottery, and gather a wide variety of plants for food, in-cluding acorns, which they laboriously ground into meal. They were still here when the Spanish came, changed their lives, obliterated their cul-ture, and named them Diegueños after the mission built to oversee their conversion. Those north of the San Diego River called themselves Ipai; south of the river were the Tipai, or Kumeyaay.

The generations of Indians who lived in the area pretty much took their natural surroundings as they found them. They lived in simple brushwood shelters, gathering what they could in season and storing the surplus for emergencies. Where there were pine trees, they gathered pine nuts. Where there were berries, they ate them, raw or cooked. When a deer or a rabbit crossed their path, they killed it with a throwing stick, used its skin for clothing, shared its meat with their extended family. In summer, when streams dried up, they went to surer water sources in the mountains, where their favorite acorn-bearing oaks were found, They lived in harmony with nature, finding nutritional, medicinal, or other uses for almost everything they encountered.

European arrivals saw things differently. Nature was meant to be tamed. Wherever they settled, they tried to make it look like where they had come from, importing plants and animals, building houses that resembled the ones they left behind. They didn't just want to adapt and survive, as the Indians had. They wanted to change their surroundings to suit their taste.

Before the Spanish came in 1769, there were no horses, cattle, or sheep, and nothing that we would call cultivation, though Indians knew how to burn an area to make it produce more abundantly the following year (see A Word About Chaparral, p. 36).

Threshing bee at the Antique Gas and Steam Engine Museum at Guajome Regional Park. Photo courtesy of the Antique Gas and Steam Engine Museum

Spanish missionaries supervised the building of the first dam and aqueduct, so they could water the wheat, olives, grapes, corn, and beans they had planted. In the quarter century of Mexican rule, the new native Californios, Spanish descendants, established huge ranchos where they raised range cattle. The hides—"California banknotes"—became San Diego's most profitable export.

After the Mexican War of 1846–47, California became U.S. territory. Once the Americans took over San Diego, they started developing it in ways the Spanish had never dreamed of—railroads, subdivisions, resorts, freeways. The rivers, dammed practically out of existence, no longer flowed freely to the sea. Unable to replenish their sands, beaches eroded, and runoff ate away the bluffs that had been here for millions of years. Pollution, the by-product of civilization, started taking its toll on plant and animal life; only by concerted effort could endangered species be saved.

Today, most of the things we take for granted here come from somewhere else. The water that turns a near-desert into a place of green lawns and tropical flowers is nearly 90 percent imported, from the Colorado River and Northern California. Oranges, originally Asian, were brought from Spain via Mexico. Avocadoes are Central American; eucalyptus trees, Australian. Our three main natural habitats—chaparral, wetlands, and streamside—have been invaded by "foreigners," who have made themselves at home, even as the rest of us non-native San Diegans have done.

As you follow our trails, consider how the area might have looked before Junipero Serra, Alonzo Horton, John D. Spreckels, Colonel Ed Fletcher, or the Scripps family came to town. Our open spaces are a blend of the natural and the civilized, what nature has supplied, and what man has added to it. They are themselves fragile things, and your continued use and support will help assure their continued existence.

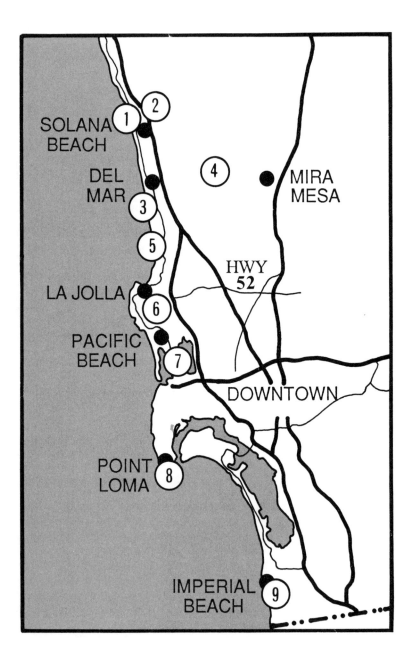

SOLANA
BEACH

DEL
MAR

LA JOLLA

PACIFIC
BEACH

POINT
LOMA

IMPERIAL
BEACH

MIRA
MESA

HWY
52

DOWNTOWN

COASTAL SAN DIEGO

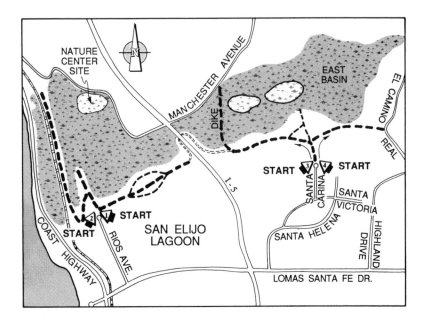

San Elijo Lagoon Ecological Reserve

◆

LOCATION:

Solana Beach.

For West Basin, Walks 1 and 2: From I-5, take Lomas Santa Fe west about 1 mile to Rios Avenue. Turn right and park at the end near the greenhouses (TB29:C3).

For East Basin, Walks 3 and 4: Take Lomas Santa Fe east to Santa Helena, just after the freeway overpass. Turn left. Then turn left again on Santa Victoria, and make one more left on Santa Carina, across from the school. Park at the end of the street (TB30:B3).

HOURS:

Always open.

DESCRIPTION:

San Elijo Lagoon is a 1000-acre wildlife reserve that is owned by the county and is popular with migratory and nesting waterfowl. Two hundred and seventy species of birds have been counted here, making the area a favorite of birdwatchers. Two man-made islands in the east basin provide safe places to nest, with the water level controlled to prohibit access by coyotes, snakes, and other predators. There are many different walks you can take in the reserve, with plant life ranging from subtropical to wetlands to chaparral. A nature center is planned for the northwest shore, off Manchester Avenue. To date there are no facilities.

HISTORY:

For thousands of years, the area around San Elijo was inhabited by Indians. All along the shores are seashell middens, or trash heaps, containing the remains of scallops, clams, and other shellfish no longer found here, since very little sea water comes into the lagoon anymore.

Until the 1880s, the lagoon had fairly good access to the ocean.

A WORD ABOUT WETLANDS

Wetlands are low-lying marshy areas that connect inland waterways to the sea. Unlike East Coast wetlands, Southern California's are generally dry in summer, and wet only when inundated by high tides, storms, or local runoff.

San Diego's coastal wetlands are primarily places of brackish water—an ever-changing mixture of salt water and fresh—that support a tremendous variety of wildlife. Our bays, lagoons, mudflats, and salt marshes provide rest stops and winter homes for over 100 species of migratory birds, and comfortable habitats for nesting ones. At low tide, thousands of these birds converge on the mudflats to make a meal of some of the crabs, clams, shrimps, snails, and worms that live there.

Wetlands are an important spawning ground for many ocean-dwelling fish. In stormy seasons, they help control flooding by acting as a buffer between the waves and the higher uplands. But, for all their usefulness, they are little appreciated.

Over 90 percent of our coastal wetlands are gone forever, dredged for harbors and marinas; filled for airports, highways, and railroads; developed into sites for hotels, power plants, shipyards, and shopping centers; diked for salt production; polluted by urban and agricultural runoff; choked by sediments from construction sites; and killed by upstream dams.

Some of Southern California's best remaining wetland areas can be found along the San Diego coast. Avid birders love these areas, but there's plenty to interest the casual walker too.

Those were the days of wide, sandy beaches, with no barriers to block the flow of sand or water.

The coming of the railroad changed all that. Trains had to have a dry, level road to run on, so a raised levee was built across the lagoon, and the course of its feeder creek was altered. This was the first step in turning a self-sufficient wetland into one that needed human intervention in order to survive.

In the 1920s, San Elijo became a kind of open cesspool, used for settling sewage. In the late 1960s, when the I-5 freeway split it in two, the lagoon was left with no way to flush itself clean. Only the bulldozers brought in from time to time to clear its silt-clogged mouth keep San Elijo from stagnating completely.

Until the 1970s, when it was acquired by the county and made into an ecological preserve, the lagoon was popular with duck hunters.

Uplands on both north and south shores have been farmed for years. In the early part of the century, drought-tolerant lima beans were the major crop; today, strawberries and trendy oriental vegetables are grown on the north side of Manchester Avenue. Although the lands here are not part of the reserve, the use of chemical pesticides and fertilizers may be a real threat to the well-being of the lagoon and its wildlife.

WEST BASIN

◆ Walk 1 The Jungle Trail

DISTANCE: 1.7 miles round trip. TIME: 45 minutes to 1 hour.

If you think our local plant life is dry, brown, and scrubby, this walk should change your mind. It's a piece of tropical rainforest in the midst of coastal chaparral, a ferny little wilderness between the wetlands and the condos.

Begin your walk on the south side of the lagoon, where Rios Street dead-ends at a luxury townhouse complex with an expansive (and expensive) view from the mountains to the sea.

Walking downhill to the right, you'll find a stand of castor bean trees, whose broadleafed branches overhang the path. Most of the year, you can see their large flower clusters and bristly red seed pods. Sometimes called the deadliest seeds on earth, no two of the intricately marked beans are alike.

As poisonous as they are, an amazing variety of products has been derived from their oil; in fact, castor oil itself is one of man's earliest commercial products. Formerly used as lamp oil and given regularly to constipated children, it is now used in high-performance engines and as a main ingredient in soaps, inks, cosmetics, plastics, nylon, paints and varnishes, insulation materials, and brake and embalming fluids. The toxin, ricin, is currently being studied as a promising cure for cancer.

The sun rarely reaches this part of the trail, so it's often damp and sometimes downright muddy. In summer, you'll notice distinct changes of humidity as you move from shaded to open areas. In spring, there's such a profusion of pastel wild radish you might think you're in an English country garden. There are also patches of orange and yellow nasturtiums, "escaped" from neighborhood gardens years ago, when people started dumping their cuttings here.

You may catch a whiff of licorice in the air before you see the tall stalks of fennel, with its ferny leaves. It is said that the padres scattered fennel on the floors of their chapels so it would perfume the air when crushed by the weight of kneeling—and certainly unwashed—supplicants. The seeds taste of licorice too, and are often served in East Indian restaurants as an after-dinner breath freshener. If you can't smell the licorice right off, try rubbing the leaves between your fingers.

This licorice smell is one of the big differences between fennel and its deadly look-alike, poison hemlock. Hemlock killed Socrates, and has done in a number of grazing cattle. There have been a few cases of humans dying too, after eating hemlock seeds mistaken for fennel, or trying the old boy scout trick of making whistles out of the hollow stalks. Poison hemlock leaves look more like carrot tops than ferns, but in winter, when both plants are dry, seed-topped stalks, the difference is harder to notice. There are a number of hemlock plants growing around the lagoon too, so unless you're absolutely positive you know what you're tasting, DON'T.

This applies equally to any mushrooms that you may find along the trail, especially after it rains. Not long ago, two Northern California students cooked, ate, and enjoyed some mushrooms they had collected; one ended up having to have a liver transplant. It's safer to look, but don't touch; some of the mushrooms here have really interesting shapes and colors.

Winter is the best time to see the profusion of bright green polypody ferns along the north-facing slopes of the path. Ferns, the descendants of ancient water plants, are usually found in moist areas. In spring, you can feel rows of tiny lumps on the backs of the fronds. These are the spores, which grow into new plants that don't look like adult ferns at all. Eventually, the almost invisible offspring produce sperm and eggs; each fertilized egg becomes a new fern. Like all of San Diego's 26 native ferns, polypody sprouts after the first fall rains, and by June is completely dried up.

The jungly part of the trail is short, but sweet. Afterwards, you'll emerge into the more typical coastal sage scrub: buckwheat, sagebrush, and sage. This was a jeep road until the early 1980s, when a heavy rainstorm sent the whole hillside sliding down in the kind of instant erosion geologists call "slope slump."

Notice the arroyo willows on the lagoon side of the trail. If you come

San Elijo Lagoon

here between January and March, you should be able to find furry "pussy willows," chartreuse catkins, yellow flowers, and fluff-covered seeds, all on the same tree. Actually, you can tell the sex of a willow by the color of its catkins—yellow for fellows, green for girls. Also in this area are acacia trees, flaunting their sneeze-provoking yellow blossoms in late winter and early spring.

Beyond the trees is a sandy clearing formed by runoff from over-watered hilltop lawns. From here, follow the lower Shoreside Trail left through the pampas grass forest, if you want to observe some of the waterbirds that make their home in the lagoon. You'll usually find a number of white-billed black coots swimming around; some people call them mudhens. Watch for their fluffy red-headed chicks in summer.

In winter, when hundreds of migratory waterbirds arrive, try to distinguish the two groups of ducks: dabblers and divers. The dabblers—red heads, pintails, shovelers, and mallards—are the ones you usually see with their tails in the air, feeding off the shallow bottom. The divers—scaup, ruddy ducks, and buffleheads—are the ones who disappear into the deeper water to search for food.

Other swimmers worth watching are the tail-less pied-billed grebes. In summer, they carry their babies on their backs and sink out of sight like submarines. Note the variety of shorebirds too: pink-legged stilts, avocets with their upcurved bills, gray willets, brown dowitchers whose beaks peck through the mud with the speed of sewing machine needles, and the beautiful long-legged waders—great blue herons, white egrets, and the iridescent black white-faced ibis.

When it rains, this lower trail may flood out, but you can usually bypass the flooded areas. There are several kinds of salt marsh plants here, even though the water is not very salty anymore. Notice the pickleweed, a low-growing succulent with tiny pickle-shaped leaves that turn red in fall. In March, in the shallows around the pickleweed, watch for the frantic activity of spawning carp, some of them 2 feet long.

The Shoreside Trail meets up with a Center Trail that goes straight through the chaparral—mostly broom, deerweed, and sagebrush. From here, you can continue east up to the freeway embankment, then head north (left), finally crossing under the freeway to the west end of Walk 3.

But we like to take the trail that forks to the right, going up through the trees of the Vanishing Forest, a grove of eucalyptus, acacia, mimosa, palms, and Monterey cypress, planted years ago as ornamentals. As time and storms take their toll, dead trees are replaced with native cottonwoods, live oaks, and willows by rangers and some of the volunteers who are actively involved in the reserve's maintenance and preservation. There are a number of offshoot paths that lead in and around the trees; look carefully and you'll find the foundations of an old farm house that once stood here.

On your left, past the wooded area, is a steep trail up to The Meadow. In spring, the slopes here are covered with golden California poppies, yellow sea dahlias, blue lupine, red paintbrush, and the picturesquely named Chinese houses. Resist the temptation to take home a bouquet; remember, this is a protected area.

Continuing west along the Upper Trail, you'll see a path uphill into Holmwood Canyon, a recent addition to the reserve. If you don't take this detour, in a few minutes you'll come to the jungle again, and be heading back to your car.

◆ Walk 2 The Pole Road Trail
DISTANCE: 1.5 miles. TIME: 45 minutes to 1 hour.

This walk is especially favored by birders, because it gives them a chance to get close to many of the birds that winter in the lagoon. Follow the dirt road down toward the water, take the path that forks to the right, and go out onto The Isthmus, a levee in the middle of the lagoon.

The higher areas that birds like to rest on are the remnants of the old sewage dikes; when the water level is low, you can see their hourglass shape. The posts occupied by terns, gulls, and cormorants mark underground gas and sewage pipelines.

There are always ducks here, and usually hawks, great blue herons, and pelicans. In early summer, you can't miss the stilts and avocets, who fly at you, shrieking, trying to frighten you away from their nests.

Return to the dirt road and follow it to the graveled Pole Road used by San Diego Gas and Electric to maintain its power lines. From here, you can go north, almost all the way to Cardiff. At the west end of the hairpin turn, there's a small path that crosses the railroad tracks and Highway 101. This is the path many locals take to the beach.

As you walk on by, you may notice the tell-tale scent of the cement block pumping station; take shallow breaths and try to ignore it. Look for green-backed herons fishing along the shore and kingfishers perched on the powerlines. Continue past the old sewage treatment plant, where we once took shelter during a sudden downpour. At the end, above and to the right of the railroad trestle, are the remains of an old kelp factory, which, during World War I, produced kelp by-products used in the manufacture of gunpowder.

EAST BASIN

Walks 3 and 4 begin at the north end of Santa Carina, east of I-5. Cross through the old lima bean fields, now covered with broom and other chaparral shrubs. You'll begin to see bits of broken shell underfoot, the scattered remains of ancient Indian seafood feasts, from the days when shellfish were still plentiful here. Leavings were heaped up and covered with dirt, before the smell became overpowering. Farmers clearing the land disturbed these kitchen middens in the early part of this century. Now walkers and gophers are uncovering them again. The origin of the bits of shell along the freeway embankment is less certain; they're part of the landfill, and might have come from anywhere.

The path forks at about 0.2 mile, near two large eucalyptus trees. Walk 3 heads west toward the freeway, and Walk 4 heads east to El Camino Real.

◆ Walk 3 Tern Point and Flood Control Dike
DISTANCE: 2 miles round trip. TIME: 45 minutes to 1 hour.

When you come to the eucalyptus trees, take the left-forking trail. There are several dead trees here that are hunting perches for kites, hawks, kingbirds, woodpeckers, and ravens, so keep your eyes open. Stay on the upper trail that leads out to Tern Point, and you'll have a good view of the entire east basin and the two islands, where avocets, killdeer, mallards, and the endangered least terns make their nests during the summer. State Fish and Game wardens have placed red roof tiles on the islands to provide shade for the nests, as many shorebirds need some shade in order for their eggs to develop.

Retrace your steps back to the main trail, heading west toward the freeway. Up ahead on the left is a deep gully, evidence of erosion by over-watered lawns and inadequate storm drains on the street above.

Notice how the chaparral plant community comes right down to meet the salt marsh. If you keep your eyes on the edge of the cattails, just at water level, you might see a Virginia rail or an American bittern, shy birds that live among the reeds.

If you continue toward the freeway, you can pick up the trail that goes along the embankment and under the overpass to connect with Walk 1, the Jungle Trail.

When the water level is low enough, you can cross the flood control dike to Manchester Avenue. Look for the tracks of raccoons in the mud, and the leftover claws of their crayfish dinners. This is another good place for birding; great blue herons and egrets like to sit on the fence waiting for a catfish, carp, or bass to swim by. You may even see a sharp-eyed osprey dive down into the water, and fly back up to a feeding perch, holding its catch like a torpedo.

◆ Walk 4 La Orilla Trail

DISTANCE: 2 miles round trip. TIME: 45 minutes to 1 hour.

Just past the north end of Santa Carina, take the right fork near the eucalyptus trees and head east toward the powerlines. Soon you'll start going downhill, past a hillside thickly covered with fuchsia-flowered gooseberry, scrub oak, bush monkey flower, cucumber vines, honeysuckle, and chaparral pea. The lagoon side of the path will give you a glimpse of many of the visiting waterfowl. One foggy morning, we saw a well-fed coyote watching for birds—just like us.

About 0.5 mile along the trail, you'll reach a flatter area where there are clumps of pale pampas grass. Introduced in the late 1800s, when huge urns full of the tall plumes were part of every fashionable Victorian drawing room, pampas grass is another escaped plant that spreads quickly and suffocates its neighbors. Digging out these clumps is a back-breaking job, but the Parks Department is getting county prisoners to do the work, which may go a long way toward convincing them that crime doesn't pay.

There are large stretches of pickleweed around here, home to the endangered savannah sparrow. In June, you'll see the showy yellow blossoms of Hooker's evening primrose, named for a botanist friend of Darwin, not a lady of easy virtue. In fall, look for goldfinches digging out seeds from the dead flower clusters.

Up ahead, under the powerlines, is a freshly planted area. In an attempt to slow down erosion, the Parks Department recently extended a storm drain and put in a good selection of native plants, with a drip irrigation system to water them.

Past the powerlines, La Orilla Trail meanders through a sandy section and finally merges with a horse trail through the marshland called Orilla Creek. The Parks Department has improved the trail, leading it to somewhat higher and drier ground, where pink alkali heath and yellow daisy-like jaumea bloom in summer. You can continue east to El Camino Real, the old Indian trail followed by Spanish soldiers and missionaries on their travels north. For a nice variation, start your walk from this end, parking near the corner of La Orilla and El Camino Real. You can go all the way to the beach following the trails we've described.

San Dieguito Park

LOCATION:

Solana Beach/Rancho Santa Fe. From I-5, take the Lomas Santa Fe exit and go east about 1 mile (TB30:C4).

Upper Entrance: From Lomas Santa Fe, go north on Highland Drive to Sun Valley Road. Turn right, then left into park.

Lower Entrance: From Lomas Santa Fe, go north on Highland to El Camino Real. Turn right; the entrance is 200 yards ahead.

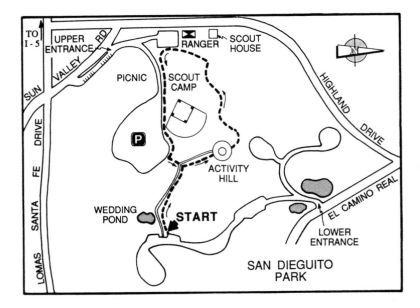

HOURS:

9:30 a.m. to sunset. $1.00 parking fee.

DESCRIPTION:

This 122-acre oasis in fast-growing North County is a great place to go for a family picnic, a morning run, or a quiet stroll. It's a combination of developed and "natural" attractions, including ballfields, horseshoe pits and playgrounds, picnic tables and barbecues, a fitness course, and an equestrian trail. Although much of the park is on hilly ground, there is handicapped access to picnic areas and restrooms. Group picnic areas, a paved dancing pavilion, and the grassy slope beside the Wedding Pond may be reserved for private parties. A youth-group campsite is also available. Call County Parks, 565-3600, for reservations.

HISTORY:

San Dieguito, "Little San Diego," was the name of a rancho established here by the first mayor of the pueblo of San Diego, Juan Maria Osuna. The area had been designated as an Indian settlement in the 1830s when Governor Figueroa started "secularizing" the missions, but Osuna, not bothering with the fine points, simply appropriated 8000 acres of the best land, acquiring a formal grant in 1845.

When he died, the rancho was inherited by his son, Leandro, who treated the Indians like slaves. They retaliated by feeding him a concoction of cactus fruit and ground human bones, reputed to cause a slow and painful death. Believing he was doomed, Leandro shot himself; some say his ghost still wanders the grounds of San Dieguito.

In 1906, a branch of the Santa Fe Railroad Company bought up all the original property and renamed it Rancho Santa Fe. Executives envisioning forests of cheap railroad ties imported three million eucalyptus seedlings from Australia. Fast-growing, drought-tolerant, and very much in vogue, eucalyptus turned out to be a disappointment; the wood warped when wet and split as soon as they drove a spike into it. The project was abandoned, but the trees remain, tall and silent witnesses to the dangers of insufficient research. Hummingbirds and orioles seem to love them anyway.

◆ The Walk

DISTANCE: 1.5 miles round trip. TIME: 45 minutes to 1 hour.

Our favorite hike starts at the lower entrance. Drive in, bear left, and park just south of the restrooms. You'll pass a pair of duck ponds, a popular hangout for what birders call "funny ducks," the half-breed offspring of wild mallards and abandoned domestic ones. Some of them will swim right up to visitors, looking for a handout; carry along a few slices of bread if you want to feed them. You can always tell the wild mallards—they're the ones who ignore you. Some days, you may also see a king-fisher, an egret, or a great blue heron.

The 1-mile fitness course starts right past the ponds. From here you get a fine view of the broad green slopes and the variety of trees found in the lower part of the park. There are sycamores, black willows, pepper trees, pomegranates, liquidambar—a red maple look-alike—and, of course, eucalyptus.

Once you've had a general look around, walk up the main road. About 100 yards from the second drainage crossing, you'll come to a dirt road on your right, with an "Authorized Vehicles Only" sign. Follow it uphill, bearing right. If you smell something sweet, it's Cleveland sage; there's a small clump on the mound where the trail forks at the top.

Still bearing right, stay on the main trail, heading toward a single tall eucalyptus. You'll see a yellow ridge of Torrey sandstone, slowly shaped under shallow seas millions of years ago and eroded by wind and rain when the water receded. There's a good vista point here, with views from the huge homes and horse paddocks of Rancho Santa Fe all the way to the mountains.

You are now on Activity Hill, an imaginative play area for children and—why not?—playful adults. Start with the bouncy swinging bridge to your right, cross the second bridge, and go on to the double log balance beams. Heading back up to the top are three big ladders; farther down is a single log balance beam. Take your choice or try them all; this a fine place to let your hair down.

When you're played out, follow the remains of the old cement slide downhill. This slide was a favorite of kids when the area was first opened. They waxed it with surfboard wax and slid down on pieces of carpet and burlap sacks, but after a number of concussions and broken arms, it was finally covered over.

Where the trail forks, go left. Look for caterpillar vine here; its leaves are fernlike and unremarkable, but in bloom, it resembles an invasion of green caterpillars.

Ahead are some coast prickly pear cacti, and farther on, a set of wooden steps; take them up to the G-to-A section of the marked nature trail. This bit of chaparral is especially pretty in late winter and spring when the red paintbrush, purple nightshade, blue-eyed grass, and bright green mosses and ferns are all at their best.

At the clearing up ahead, you can see telegraph weed, the tall Hooker's evening primrose, and tree tobacco, a South American import too poisonous to smoke, but used by local Indians to treat rheumatism and swollen glands.

Swinging bridge at Activity Hill. Photo by Barbara Moore

If you want, try the H-to-O section of trail to your right. It's less interesting than the previous section, mostly just buckwheat, black sage, and broom, but it's a short walk and not unpleasant.

Broom, by the way, is often found in areas once cleared for farming. Seventy-five years ago, Solana Beach was covered with acres of lima beans, a crop that needed no irrigation, an important consideration in water-starved Southern California. Broom has taken over these lower, flatter places where beans once grew; higher, steeper locations are virtually broomless.

From the clearing, bear left to the service road, then take a left and go past the Scout Camp and Scout House, designed for tenderfoot campers whose outdoor experience may include a dip in the pool of the country club across the street.

Now you're back in civilization again, with playgrounds, restrooms, a ballfield, and a group picnic area just ahead. The ranger office is here, and also an information kiosk. Up the hill to your right are more picnic and play areas, and the Upper Entrance. This is a good time to stop for

A Word About Chaparral

Chaparral, the most common plant community in San Diego, is as typical of the area as pine forests are of the mountains. It takes its name from a Mexican word for scrub oak: *chaparro* meaning "shorty." Nineteenth century *vaqueros*—Mexican cowboys—invented the protective leg coverings called chaps when they grew tired of beating their way through the brambles while rounding up stray cattle. Originally, even their horses wore chaps.

Chaparral is often referred to as coastal sage scrub, although strictly speaking, chaparral is the taller, evergreen stuff, like lemonade berry and laurel sumac. Sage scrub tends to be shorter, more aromatic, and have softer leaves, like sagebrush. Some naturalists call the whole community an "elfin forest"—a pretty term for a group of short trees and bushes that are forest enough for the small animals living among them.

Chaparral plants are *opportunistic,* which means they take advantage of the slightest rainfall to bloom, drop their seeds, and carry on the species. They have to be tough to survive the long dry periods in Southern California. All year long, they hoard water in their small waxy leaves and deep roots. In summer, when there's almost no water to be had, most of them lie dormant, just as some animals hibernate to survive the winter. During this time, they can catch fire easily, and the flames spread... well, like wildfire. Afterwards, the land may look dead and bare, but the first drops of rain bring an amazing burst of new life.

Brush fires are actually good for the chaparral. Some plants inhibit the growth of others, and fire clears out areas so new plants can grow. It also gets rid of dead wood and gives certain seeds the conditions they need for sprouting. Some seeds may wait in the ground for years until a fire cracks their tough outer coatings enough to make them susceptible to the next rainfall. The early natives of San Diego knew this, and often set fire to an area they expected to return to later on, assuring themselves of a good harvest.

Chaparral plants have another interesting way of dealing with fire. Just weeks after a blaze has turned shrubs into charred skeletons, green shoots start springing up from the underground burls that escaped the heat of the flames. This kind of plant reincarnation is called *crown sprouting.*

One final word: If you come from a place of tall trees or green meadows, you may think chaparral is the kind of stuff only a botanist could love. You'll probably find it dry and disappointing at first, but the more you know about it, the more it will grow on you. Promise.

lunch, or try a new activity.

When you're ready to leave, take the dirt road from the upper parking lot and walk east. Bear right at the fork, and continue downhill, passing the small Wedding Pond, till you're back on the paved road again. Or, if you're still game, try any of the small trails branching off into the "bush."

Some of these paths are so overgrown, you'll feel as if you're out in the middle of nowhere. If you're lucky, you might see a family of California quail. If not, you'll have something to look forward to on your next visit.

Torrey Pines State Reserve
◆

LOCATION:

Del Mar/ La Jolla.

Main Reserve

From I-5, take the Carmel Valley Road exit and go west to the light at North Torrey Pines Road. Turn left, cross Peñasquitos Lagoon, and look for the entrance road 0.5 mile on your right. Drive uphill and park near the lodge (TB34:A6).

East Grove

Flintkote Road: From I-5, take Carmel Valley Road west to Sorrento Valley Road. Turn left and continue to the light at Sorrento Valley Boulevard. Turn right, then right again onto Roselle. Stay on Roselle until it dead-ends on Estuary. Turn left, then turn right onto Flintkote. Follow the rutted road for just over a mile, passing the ranger's residence about halfway. Park in the small dirt parking area, near a "No Dogs/Vehicles/Camping" sign and a bright yellow trash can. (TB38:B2).

Torrey Pines Extension

Del Mar Scenic Parkway: From I-5, take the Carmel Valley Road exit and go west to Del Mar Scenic Parkway, just opposite the North Beach parking lot. Turn right and continue on to the end of the street. Park near the tennis court (TB34:B5).

Mira Montana: From I-5, take the Del Mar Heights Road exit and go west to Mercado. Turn left, then left again onto Cordero. Go two blocks and turn right on Mira Montana. Drive through the iron gate and park in the small parking area (TB34:B4).

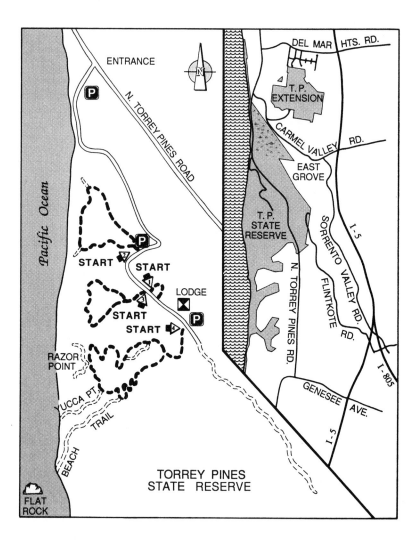

HOURS:

Main reserve, 9:00 a.m. to sunset. $4.00 day-use fee. Visitor's Lodge, 11 a.m. to 4 p.m. East Grove and the Extension are always open; no fee.

DESCRIPTION:

"Torrey Pines State Reserve is a majestic wilderness island amidst an increasingly urban area," says the visitor's guide, and so it is. It includes about 2000 acres of spectacular cliffs, canyons, mesas, beaches, and wetlands spread out over three locations.

The 1000-acre main reserve has the greatest concentration of Torrey pines, over 3000 of them. These rare trees are found in only one other location: on Santa Rosa Island, off Santa Barbara.

At park headquarters in the visitor's lodge, there are interactive displays of some of the animals and birds that live in the reserve, and a small but interesting bookshop. A board outside the office gives weekly information on what's in bloom. In front of the lodge is a labeled native plant garden where you can check your knowledge. Volunteers offer excellent slide shows and guided walks on weekends at 11:30 a.m. and 1:30 p.m. The park can get really crowded on weekend afternoons; try to come early, or during the week.

There are restrooms and drinking fountains across from the lodge's parking lot. Outside the main reserve, there are no facilities.

HISTORY:

Centuries ago, Indians came here to gather seeds from the cones of the Torrey pines. Spanish explorers, noticing this was the only tree-covered section of coastline in the area, named it Punta de los Arboles or "Tree Point." American navigators used it as a landmark, calling it Pine Hill.

In 1850, the year California became a state, Dr. C. C. Parry, official botanist for the U.S.-Mexican boundary survey, identified the Torrey pine as a new species. He named it after his friend, botanist John Torrey.

Unique and hardy, the Torrey pine gradually acquired staunch supporters among local conservationists. By 1885, it was a criminal offense to cut down any of the trees, which picnickers had been using for firewood.

In 1899, the city of San Diego established 369 acres as a public park. Philanthropist Ellen Browning Scripps began buying land to the north to add to the park, and in 1921, she appointed Guy Fleming custodian of the newly named Torrey Pines Reserve.

Fleming, a dedicated conservationist and park administrator, had worked on the planning and planting of Balboa Park. Later, as District Supervisor of State Parks, he oversaw the development of Anza-Borrego, Palomar Mountain, Cuyamaca, and Coronado's Silver Strand. The home he built on the reserve is used today as a ranger residence. In 1923, the Torrey Pines Lodge was opened as a restaurant and gift shop and became a regular tour bus lunch stop. It is now the park's headquarters and the site of its small museum.

Ownership of the reserve was transferred to the state of California in the 1950s. One hundred acres were set aside at the south end for construction of a public golf course. Continued public interest and support have added Torrey Pines Extension, Peñasquitos Lagoon, and other small parcels to the original park acreage.

Needles and cones

MAIN RESERVE

The main reserve has a number of well-maintained trails that are beautiful all year long. All distances are round trip from the lodge, where trail maps are always available.

◆ Walk 1 High Point Trail

DISTANCE: 0.7 mile round trip. TIME: 15 minutes.

As its name implies, this is the highest point in the reserve, with a commanding view eastward across the lagoon to distant Black Mountain, and westward to La Jolla and the ocean. Rangers call this the "100-yard walk," and the climb up to the High Point bench is just about that. The walk along the road from the lodge to the trailhead is longer than the trail itself; you'd do well to combine this with another trail.

Across from the trailhead is a large Torrey pine with an odd, dense clump of needles that looks like a huge nest. Actually, it's an abnormality called "witch's broom," which may be a virus, a genetic disorder, or a kind of tree wart. There are several more examples within the reserve, but this is the most noticeable.

◆ Walk 2 Guy Fleming Trail
DISTANCE: 1.3 miles round trip. TIME: 45 minutes.

This was park supervisor Fleming's favorite walk, named in his honor after he died. To reach the trailhead, walk 0.25 mile down the road from the lodge, or park at the closer North Grove parking lot. A spring wildflower calendar/map, available for 25 cents at the lodge's bookshop, is nice to have in hand, especially from February to July, when most plants are blooming.

We like to start out by going due west, where the trail winds around a canyon wall. Two ocean overlooks provide good vantage points for watching playful dolphins and, in winter, the southward migration of California gray whales. Sometimes you can spot "rafts" of sleeping sea lions, their flippers held out of the water to catch the warmth of the sun.

Notice how the trees in this area are bent nearly to the ground, beaten down by the constant wind and salt air. After the crest of the hill, the trees stand tall and upright again, because they're more protected.

Just before the end of the trail is a birdbath, with a bench across the way. If you sit quietly for awhile, you may see a fox or a deer coming around for a drink, or more often, a scrub jay or a finch dropping in for a dip.

◆ Walk 3 The Parry Grove Trail
DISTANCE: 0.75 mile round trip. TIME: 20 to 30 minutes.

Named for the botanist who named the Torrey pines, this trail is the shadiest in the reserve. The trailhead is on your left, just across the road from High Point. A labeled native plant garden introduces you to some of the plants you'll see along the way. In spring, near the back-to-back benches, look for low-growing scarlet pimpernel. Really a coral color, these tiny flowers are called the "poor man's weatherglass" because they close up when the weather turns cloudy.

To your right, just past the benches, is a hedge of Cleveland sage, which has the nicest scent and the prettiest blue flowers of all the sages. Once it grew wild over the hills of Del Mar; now, with so much land cleared for new housing, it's almost disappeared.

Walk down the 100-plus steps descending steeply into the canyon. After passing a usually empty trail guide box, the trail flattens out and circles back, allowing some good ocean views. Then you reach the trail guide box again, and have to head back up all those steps.

◆ Walk 4 Beach Trail/Razor Point Trail Circuit

DISTANCE: 2 miles round trip. TIME: 1 to 1.5 hours.

Our very favorite hike in the reserve is really a combination of trails. Start out just north of the restrooms, following the sign to the Beach Trail, a mile-long route that's popular with local runners.

As you walk (or run) along, notice how the chaparral shrubs look as neat as if a gardener had trimmed them; this, too, is caused by the wind and salt air that mow down the plants on exposed slopes. The next part of the trail is especially pretty in spring, when there are often over 50 different kinds of wildflowers in bloom on a single day.

Just before the second bench on the trail, you'll reach a junction. The steps just ahead lead down about 0.25 mile past spectacular views of cliffs and sea to Torrey Pines Beach. Getting onto the sand involves negotiating a few yards of narrow cliffside trail near the end, so watch your step. From here, you can walk south to Black's Beach, admiring the cliffs from below. If you don't feel sure-footed enough to go all the way down, you can still enjoy the view before heading back to the bench junction.

With or without the beach interlude, go west from the junction to the Yucca Point sign. Follow it left to the overlook, where you'll see one of the largest concentrations of Mojave yucca in the reserve, plus a few narrow-leafed Whipple's yuccas. Look for the giant asparagus stalks in early spring, followed by white flower clusters and, finally, pickle-shaped seed pods.

Returning to the main trail, take the first left and head north past Big Basin, a wide bowl bordered by red badlands cliffs carved by eons of storm runoff. Stop on the small wooden bridge and look down into the narrow canyon where, in spring, there are patches of bright green ferns clinging to the pale yellow sandstone. Ahead, the trail forks left to the Razor Point overlooks, and more dramatic views of the coast.

Keeping to the main trail, you'll soon reach the first of five fenced overlooks into the Canyon of the Swifts. You might see a swift or two in spring or summer. If so, watch carefully; they have the unique habit of mating on the wing.

The dead trees you may see along the trail are the result of a recent infestation of hungry beetles that drill their way through to the inner bark and often prove fatal to drought-weakened trees. Farther along are the only native orchids we know of in the coastal area, a few stalks of tiny green flowers. They're no match for Hawaiian orchids, but it's amazing they can grow here at all.

At the next overlook, scan the canyon's small caves for great horned owls, ravens, and swifts, all of which like to nest here in spring. This part of the canyon is split by the Carmel Valley earthquake fault, a branch of the Rose Canyon fault system that runs along I-5, up Ardath Road, and out past the La Jolla Beach and Tennis Club. Longtime residents remember the old trail at the canyon's bottom, so narrow it was called Fat Man's Misery.

The path winds away and then back along the canyon, climbing steadily. (If looking down bothers you, there's a small trail to the right just before the third overlook that leads up over Red Butte, connecting with the main trail once the canyon's safely behind you.) At the top of the steps bear left; the right-hand trail leads up to Red Butte. Soon you'll come to the first part of the beach trail. Go left, and it won't be long until you're back at the restrooms across from the lodge.

EAST GROVE

◆ Walk 5

DISTANCE: 4 miles round trip to beach. TIME: 1.5 to 2 hours.

This is a good, get-away-from-it-all trail. You will hear the distant sound of traffic, and occasionally, a train will pass close enough to let you wave to the engineer, but you'll probably have the place to yourself. After heavy rain or if Peñasquitos Lagoon is full, your walk here will be a lot shorter; the trail could flood out after the first half mile or so.

Follow the path toward the cliffs through the sagebrush, fennel, and telegraph weed. In spring, among the wildflowers, look for orange fiddleneck, which kids used to whisper would make you wet your bed at night if you touched it. To your left above the chaparral, you'll see a few Torrey pines. There were more until 1972, when an angry young man disappointed in love set the grove on fire. Subsequent planting of rye grass for erosion control actually inhibited the regrowth of native plants and trees.

The tall pale bluffs, pockmarked by eons of erosion, are part of the Torrey sandstone whose formation began forty million years ago. Today, owls and ravens like to nest in the small cavelike hollows.

After half a mile, the trail dips down and the vegetation changes; you'll see water-loving plants like alkali heath, pickleweed, and salt grass. When the lagoon is full, this may be as far as you can go. As you round the point across from the railroad trestle, notice the white "icing" in the dried mud. If you were to taste it (yuck!) you'd know what it is in a second—salt. This is a salt marsh, and all the plants here have to be able to tolerate a lot of salt in their soil.

Look up on the hillside to your left; the bits of white shell sticking out are the remains of ancient La Jollan Indian kitchen middens, or trash heaps. Pay attention to the tall clumps of round reed; those long, pointed

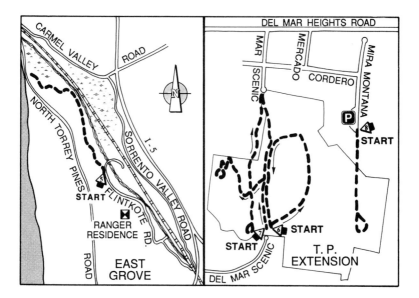

quills can tattoo your legs if you're not careful.

We call this the "animal track trail" because deer, coyote, and raccoon tracks can almost always be found here. Animals come here daily to drink from Peñasquitos Creek, and even if you never get to see them, you can learn a lot from studying their tracks. Coyotes, for example, walk a straight line, one paw in front of the other, unlike dogs or other animals. Deer step with their hind feet almost in the same spot as their front feet. Raccoon tracks look like the handprints of human babies.

In drier months, you can follow this trail through the pickleweed all the way to the beach. Your energy and the lagoon's water level will determine the turnaround point.

THE EXTENSION

Twenty-five years ago, the Extension was well on its way to becoming another condominium complex. Developers had already cleared a road through the valley, cut down several trees, and installed a storm drain before a determined citizen's group raised enough money to save the land. Despite some permanent damage, primarily the turning of a seasonal stream into a deep erosion gully, the Extension is today a quiet and lovely place to walk, even after rain.

A wide valley separates two distinctly different upland areas. The eastern section, Trail A, is drier and has few trees, while the western ridge, Trail B and the D.A.R. trail system, offers pine-shaded ocean views.

◆ Walk 6 Margaret Fleming Trail A

DISTANCE: 0.75 mile round trip. TIME: 45 minutes.

Just after you enter the Extension, two signs mark trails named for Guy Fleming's wife. Born Margaret Doubleday Eddy, she was a wealthy New Jersey debutante, the niece of Abner Doubleday, who invented modern baseball. On a visit to La Jolla, she fell in love with Fleming, and soon gave up East Coast society for San Diego's great outdoors. Her nature etchings and lithographs were widely exhibited, and she was one of the major forces in the Extension's acquisition.

Trail A begins at the right fork, gradually climbing through black sage, sagebrush, and bush sunflower. The lone Torrey pine you see just after the wooden steps shows the black scars of a fire that swept through here in 1962. Numbered markers are the remains of an old nature trail for which guides are no longer available.

At #18, near a "tunnel" of laurel sumac, is a woodrats' nest; it's on the right, and looks like a large pile of dry, brown sticks. Woodrats, sometimes called packrats, are nocturnal animals that build elaborate nests with separate bedrooms, bathrooms, pantries, and nurseries. There are a number of these nests in the Extension, some of them hundreds of years old.

Farther along on your right, look for the bright yellow blossoms of tree poppy among the shorter bush sunflowers. Tree poppy usually grows in disturbed areas, especially after fires. After you pass through another

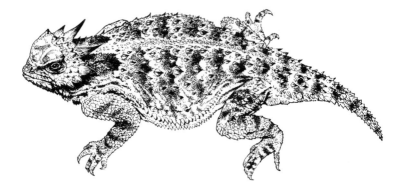

San Diego horned lizard. Drawing by David Stump

"tunnel" of ceanothus (#16), there's some bee plant, whose large toothed leaves and tiny red blossoms are noticeable in spring. Despite its name, we've never seen any bees hovering around it.

At #15, there are several toyon, whose red berries start appearing in late fall. Near #14, you'll see spice bush, our native citrus. Some people are allergic to its oil, which can make the skin hypersensitive to sun. The fruits look like tiny oranges.

A bit farther on is yerba santa, the "holy herb," whose pale fuzzy leaves are sometimes called "nature's bandaids." In spring, clusters of lavender flowers improve its odd, ungainly appearance.

A set of wooden stairs will take you past a dense stand of scrub oak (#11) and onto a sandstone ridge that leads to a chamise-covered mesa.

Keeping the red rock outcroppings on your right, head north on the path through the shrubs. In early spring, you'll see and smell a field of wild onions. Toward May, the area is pink with low-growing canchalagua, whose bright star-shaped flowers like the dry hard soil here.

As you approach the fenced schoolyard, watch out for the small, round rocks called concretions. These ironstone ballbearings, formed underwater ages ago, can trip you up if you're not careful.

Walk down more steps, passing clumps of yellow rockrose in spring, and showy scarlet larkspur in June. Hummingbirds love the larkspur, and this is one of the few places in the county where it is found. There's lots more yerba santa here, and the trail is somewhat eroded and overgrown. Follow the erosion gully around and over the roots to a Torrey pine, the one on the hill, about 100 feet to the left. The Torrey pine's root system can extend out hundreds of feet in its search for water.

Walking down the gully, which widens into a wash, you'll pass a number of gabions, rock-filled wire cages designed to slow erosion, but not terribly effective. Follow the wash back down to the entrance, or take one of the small paths that lead off to the right and connect with Trail B.

◆ Walk 7 Margaret Fleming Trail B and the D.A.R. Trail System

DISTANCE: Up to 2 miles round trip. TIME: 45 minutes to 1 hour.

From the trailhead, follow Trail B to your left, avoiding the wash. Take your first left, to a series of wooden steps, another form of erosion control. They lead uphill to the western ridge and the D.A.R. trail system, funded by the California Daughters of the American Revolution. Along this path, you'll pass white sage, wild cucumber, Mojave yuccas, and, in early spring, yellow sea dahlias. At the top of the ridge, there's a panoramic view of the ocean.

Here you have three choices:

1. Go left along the ridge to a cul-de-sac that overlooks the lagoon, the main reserve, and the ocean. This is a great place to be at sunset; there's even a bench to sit on.

2. Follow the fence to your right, heading down some steps and into a tree-lined trail with the piney smell of the Sierras. Look for purple snapdragon and red Indian pinks here in spring. There's another bench just before you cross the wooden bridge and go left, down a steep flight of steps into a small canyon. (Straight ahead is private property.)

Steps lead up again to a short loop around a little knoll. Several years ago, a small control burn was conducted here, to see how fire affects the germination of seeds and the birth of new Torrey pines. Nothing much was learned, but you can still see the burnt bark on the trees.

3. A sharp right leads away from the ridge-top fence and up along the main D.A.R. trail. While you admire the view, keep an eye out for coast horned lizards, those endangered miniature dinosaurs that tend to blend in with their surroundings and are generally sand-colored here.

The trail rises slightly, then goes down more steps past summer-blooming sand aster, lavender flowers with yellow centers. After the steps, as the trail flattens out and heads north, look for an enormous woodrats' nest on your left; this one must be many years old.

Passing toyon and yerba santa, you'll soon come to a junction. Straight up the hill is Mar Scenic Drive, an alternative entrance to the Extension. Downhill to the right is the trail to follow if you want to go out the way you came in. Note the remnants of the old blacktop along the path; if not for conservationists, this would have been Del Mar Scenic Parkway.

◆ Walk 8 Mira Montana Entrance: The Red Ridge Trail

DISTANCE: 1 mile round trip. TIME: 30 minutes.

This sandy trail is popular with local runners and after-work dog-walkers. From the parking area, walk south a few hundred yards to the metal gate. Inside, on the left, are several large clumps of fragrant Cleveland sage.

Where the trail divides around a stand of Torrey pines, look for biscuit root, a member of the carrot family, whose pale yellow spring flowers turn to maroon seed-pod clusters that dry to beige in early summer. Though considered inedible, it got its name from explorers Lewis and Clark, who ate the roots of a similar plant, and thought it tasted like stale biscuits.

As you walk on you'll get a bird's-eye view of the incredible spread of development to the east. To the west is the more restful sight of the sea.

From May to July, if you think you smell a skunk, look for skunkweed, a ground-hugging thistlelike plant with small lavender flowers. Nearby you should also see pink Turkish rugging and green mats of tread lightly, two other short, prickly plants.

Take the trail to its southern end, a red ridge overlooking a rugged canyon, then circle back along the eastern rim.

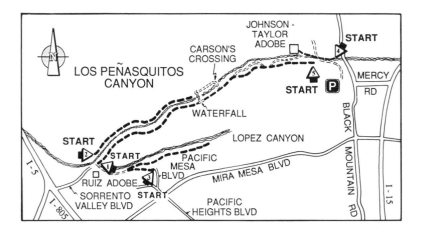

Los Peñasquitos Canyon Preserve

LOCATION:

Sorrento Valley/Mira Mesa.

West End—Sorrento Valley: Take I-5 north to Carmel Valley Road. Go west to Sorrento Valley Road. Turn left and continue to Sorrento Valley Boulevard. Turn left again at the light and go to the end. Park as close to the end of the street as you can—the preserve starts there (TB38:E3).

Lopez Canyon—Sorrento Mesa: Take I-805 north to Mira Mesa Boulevard. Go east to Pacific Heights Boulevard; turn left. At the next light, Pacific Mesa Boulevard, turn right. Go to the end and park (TB39:A3).

East End—Peñasquitos/Mira Mesa: Take I-15 north to Mercy Road. Go west to Black Mountain Road and the entrance of the park (TB35:F6).

HOURS:

West End and Lopez Canyon are always open. East End, 8:00 a.m. to sunset.

DESCRIPTION:

One of our favorite locations for long and short hikes is Los Peñasquitos Canyon Preserve, with its meadows, tree-lined trails, and wide-open spaces. This 2500-acre natural park, jointly owned by city and county, was invaded in early 1988 by developers who built a 20-foot-high vehicle road from the west entrance to Lopez Ridge. It's still a fine place to walk, though, and popular with mountain bikers and horseback riders too. There are creeks to cross, shallow pools to cool your feet in, even a little waterfall. Seven miles long from end to end, the canyon is a haven for wildlife. There are no facilities.

HISTORY:

The canyon called Los Peñasquitos, "the little cliffs," was the first private land grant in San Diego County. In 1823, 10 years before the missions were secularized and their properties divided, 8000 acres of good grazing land were given to Presidio Commander Francisco Maria Ruiz. At 76, Ruiz, who had built the first house in Old Town, built the first house outside it, near the west end of the canyon. Unmarried, he moved in with the family of his friend, Francisco Maria Alvarado, who looked after him until his death 10 years later. Before he died, he transferred the entire property to Alvarado.

In 1846, the rancho was the first rest stop for General Kearny's battered Army of the West after the Battle of San Pasqual. Knowing Alvarado's anti-American sympathies, Kearny's men raided his land for cattle, food, and supplies. Alvarado's daughter ended up marrying an American, Colorado River boat captain, George Alonzo Johnson. The ranch house Johnson built near Black Mountain Road is now the ranger station.

In the 1880s, Jacob Shell Taylor, developer of old Del Mar, bought the rancho and converted the house into a hotel. Afterwards, cattle interests took over the property, and the original buildings were used as bunk houses for ranch hands.

The county acquired the 200 acres around the Johnson-Taylor Adobe in 1974, and the lion's share of the property was purchased by the city a few years later. It was established as a preserve in 1980.

WEST END

Park where you can—quite a problem on weekdays, during business hours, when employees and customers of the high-tech companies on the street take up most of the spaces. Walk in through the vehicle gate, along the raised embankment, soon to be a major road. At about 0.1 mile, a small path leads down to the pedestrian gate. Cattle grazed here for 150 years, until the city council banned them from the canyon in June 1989. We don't miss the cowpies, but we do miss the cows—they gave us a real sense of rancho history.

To the right are the remains of the oldest house in North County, the Ruiz-Alvarado Adobe; just beyond is an old corral that, until recently, was used for inoculating cattle.

In spring, in the creek, there are masses of yellow iris blooming, and you can often see egrets and great blue herons searching for crayfish. Many red-winged blackbirds make their nests in the creekside cattails; watch for males enthusiastically displaying their red shoulder patches during breeding season.

Starting from the adobe, you have a choice of two trails.

◆ Walk 1 The Road to Yuma

DISTANCE: 6 miles round trip. TIME: 3 to 3.5 hours.

One hundred and fifty years ago, wagons loaded with supplies traveled this road from San Diego to army posts at Yuma. Now it's the most popular trail in the canyon, enjoyed by joggers, horseback riders, mountain bikers, birders, and ordinary strollers all year long.

Just past the adobe is a freshwater marsh, one of the few places where you can really find snipe, wintering shorebirds that are more active on cloudy days. They have a distinctive flight pattern, zig-zagging close to the ground.

After the first rise, about 1.5 miles in, you'll see some of the palisades of volcanic rock that give Peñasquitos its name. Look over the side to see chaparral ferns and red-flowered dudleya hugging the north-facing rocks. About 3 miles in from the entrance is the waterfall. It's no Niagara, and only a trickle in summer, but it's always a nice place to relax for awhile. If you're feeling ambitious, continue on to Black Mountain Road, another 4 miles ahead.

◆ Walk 2 Meadow to Waterfall Trail

DISTANCE: 6 miles round trip. TIME: 3 to 3.5 hours.

A short way past the adobe, you'll usually find a board "bridge" over the creek, most easily crossed in summer and fall when the water level is low. Otherwise, walk along the main trail to the creek crossing near the 5-mile marker. (Usually you can hop across the creek holding onto the willows and mulefat.) The walk is well worth either inconvenience; it's one of the flattest, least traveled, and prettiest trails in the canyon.

On the north side of the creek, follow the cowpath across the meadow. Along the creekbed are trees typical of the streamside community: willows, sycamores, elderberries, and one of the few coast live oaks in this end of the canyon. In winter and early spring, when the sycamores are still bare, you can see the large stick nests of hawks and owls; each year a different pair of birds appropriates a nest. If you're tempted to stretch out at the foot of one of the trees, think again; there's lots of poison oak twining around the trunks.

Peñasquitos Canyon, West End

The south-facing slopes you pass are drier than the north-facing ones because they're not as protected from the sun. Some of them are covered with brownish green jojoba, an ingredient in shampoos and cosmetics. Because it produces a very fine oil, local conservationists tried to grow it commercially a few years back, but jojoba needs more care than they expected, and they soon gave up.

In May, near the creek, hedges of wild roses start blooming. They smell wonderful and look just like old-fashioned pink tea roses.

At about 1.5 miles, you'll come to more peñasquitos. This green-colored rock is part of a volcanic island chain formed underwater 140 million years ago. Standing on the ridge, you can see in the distance the rock outcropping where the waterfall is, about another 1.5 miles ahead. Just before the waterfall is a cement bridge. After crossing, you can head down to the water, cross over the rocks, have a little R and R, and take the main trail back. Or you can continue on about a mile to Carson's Crossing, named for frontier scout Kit Carson, who fought in the Battle of San Pasqual, a brief comedy of errors that ended in American defeat.

After the battle, Carson and two other volunteers made their way past mounted Californio sentries, crawling part of the way, to get help from San Diego for Kearny's exhausted troops, reduced to eating their mounts at Mule Hill, near what is now Rancho Bernardo. He may well have crossed here; you can take off your shoes for the same short wade and then follow the main road back to Sorrento Valley, or continue east to Black Mountain Road.

LOPEZ CANYON

In the 1840s, this canyon area was given as a land grant to Bonifacio Lopez, a master horseman who liked to take the hills at a gallop, despite his weight of 300 pounds. His descendants lived in the house he built for over 100 years.

From the "Lopez Canyon" sign, there's a nice view eastward across the canyon to Black Mountain, with the ever-developing community of Peñasquitos climbing up its base. To the south is Mt. Woodson, with Mira Mesa in the foreground.

You can take the mile loop along the rim, a flat, easy walk along a lightly graveled road. Directly across the canyon is the Wildlife Corridor, a tunnel installed by developers to provide a passage between Peñasquitos and Lopez canyons. So far, there's no evidence of animals actually using this little hole in the wall, but time will tell.

In spring, the south-facing hillsides are covered with yellow mustard, which in wet years can grow up to 6 feet tall. A cabbage relative, mustard can bloom from late winter to midsummer. Legend has it that mustard was introduced by the padres, who scattered seeds so the flowers would mark their trail as they traveled from mission to mission. The seeds are used to make the yellow spread we put on our hot dogs.

Despite the new road, you can still walk into Lopez Canyon from the west end of Peñasquitos, a flatter approach.

◆ Walk 3 Lopez Road
DISTANCE: 3.5 miles round trip. TIME: 2 hours.

To enter the canyon, take the old Lopez Road down to the rancho. You'll pass fennel, elderberry, horehound, fuchsia-flowered gooseberry, wild cucumber, and, in spring, fields of buttercups. Descending, you'll leave behind the roar of jets from nearby Miramar Air Station and the whirring of model planes sent off from the mesa top by local enthusiasts and start to hear the chirping of crickets, the creaking of tree frogs, and the trill of meadowlarks.

At the bottom, where the road forks, go right. Here are sycamores, with clumps of mistletoe hanging from their branches. Mistletoe berries are a favorite food of many birds who help spread this parasite by leaving behind droppings full of seeds. In spring, hawks and owls like to nest in the sycamores; keep an eye out for their large stick nests, and you might see a parent bird feeding its young or pushing a fledgling off a branch to teach it to hunt.

Head east along the creek, a pleasantly babbling brook in winter, a dry, cobbled streamed in summer. The jeep road you're following crisscrosses the creek, impassable after heavy rains. In spring, look for tadpoles in the still ponds; in summer, they turn into the tiny green tree frogs sometimes called "Hollywood frogs" because they can be heard on the soundtracks of so many films and TV shows shot on location in Southern California.

You can proceed through the barbed wire fence if you want. The road becomes more and more cobbly, and, after the pepper trees, drier and less interesting, but you can walk on for another 3 miles, and have a better chance of seeing deer, coyotes, or rattlers than another human. The trail comes to an end at Montongo Street in Mira Mesa.

EAST END

The entrance here was specially designed for horse trailers; ordinary cars are asked to park in the upper paved area. The main trail, a maintenance road now used by the water department, follows the old stage road to Yuma. All walks start at the gate just past the information kiosk north of the caretaker's mobile home.

On the north side of Peñasquitos Creek, invisible from here, is Canyonside Park, with its tennis courts, ballfields, and restrooms. A surge of recent development has made the area a lot less rural than it used to be, but the east end's charms will soon make you forget the suburban invasion.

After winter rains, the road may be muddy, but that's the best time to look for tracks of deer, coyote, raccoons, and, of course, horses. There are stables across the street at Horseman's Park, where horses were once for rent before insurance rates sky-rocketed. Owners still board horses there, a convenient location for trail rides.

◆ Walk 4 Adobe Trail

DISTANCE: 2 miles round trip. TIME: 1 hour.

Go west along the main road until the first right-hand fork at 0.2 mile. Take this fork, a prettier route, which intersects a crossroad at about 0.5 mile. Go right to the creek and use the south-to-north stepping stones; you won't get your feet *too* wet.

Once across, go north a few feet to rejoin the dirt crossroad. Take the first clearly defined path to the left, which leads past the overflow parking lot to an open area and the old ranch house and barn.

The Johnson-Taylor adobe, covered with plaster and wood, now houses the ranger office and resource center, open only by special arrangement. At present, tours are scheduled at 11:00 a.m. and 12:00 noon on the first and third Saturdays of every month.

On the creek side of the adobe are several huge pepper and palm trees that could be as old as the house itself. Down by the creek are an old stone springhouse, used to store perishables in pre-refrigerator days, a wooden shed, and a leaky stone cistern with a new roof. Nearby is the recent grave of a caretaker's pet, with a touching memorial. Owls like to roost in the trees here—look for their fur-ball pellets on the ground.

Just past the cistern are the remains of an old fence. Stay close to the willows and you'll see a path leading down to a board crossing of a narrow part of the creek. For a more adventurous return, follow the narrow path past the burbling creek, through a grassy clearing. Just ahead, you'll have to cross a short stretch that can get pretty muddy in winter—step lively here and you won't sink in up to your shoelaces. Stay close to the

Crossing Peñasquitos Creek. Photo by Barbara Moore

creek and continue on the path till you get to the creek crossing—you can always get the mud off your shoes there.

Alternatively, go back exactly the way you came. Either way, you'll cross the creek, pick up the vehicle road again, and bear left on the main road near sewer standpipe #86. The entrance is about 0.5 mile away. If you want to walk on, turn right at the main road, and pick up Walk 5.

◆ Walk 5 Woodland to Waterfall Trail

DISTANCE: 9 miles round trip. TIME: 3.5 to 4 hours.

This is our favorite walk in the canyon, a beautifully wooded trail with a secluded feeling, quite different from the open-range country of the west end. Here you'll get a real sense of streamside San Diego, a leafy oasis of small groves and meadows in the midst of the dry chaparral. Those 9 miles may sound long, but they are lovely, and you can stop at any of the groves along the way if you don't want to go the whole distance.

Take the main road from the gate, passing the first crossroad and continuing west. At the next fork, you can bear left to a fallen live oak tree, one of the largest in the preserve. It died of root rot, caused by runoff from the houses above. Nearby is the gravestone of John Eichar, a cook on the ranch here a century ago. Evidently, he's still remembered; there's usually a bouquet of fresh or dried flowers left on his grave.

You can sit on the dead live oak amid the fennel, horehound, and elderberry, and meditate on the cycle of life and death in the canyon. Just keep out of the poison oak.

On the road again—any one will do, but we usually choose the one closest to the creek—the next long stretch is shaded by eucalyptus, sycamores, live oaks, palms, willows, and mulefat. Look for flashy black-and-white acorn woodpeckers who use the dead snags of sycamores as acorn pantries. An entire woodpecker family will maintain a storage tree for years, sometimes making as many as 20,000 holes in one tree. In late fall and winter, keep an eye out for red-eyed phainopeplas, foraging among the red berries of toyon—the California holly.

Just past standpipe #81 on your left, a narrow trail forks off to the right, winding in and out of the trees. This is a pretty section of trail and follows the creek until it rejoins the main road at about 2 miles.

At 3.5 miles, you reach Carson's Crossing. You can dip your feet in the creek here, or stop for a picnic—we usually press on to the waterfall, continuing ever westward, bearing right at the fork under the powerlines.

At about 4.5 miles, you'll see a rock outcropping at the top of the rise ahead. That's where the waterfall is, and you're almost there. When you reach the 4-mile marker, you'll have actually walked over 4.7 miles. Go right here and follow the path down to the edge of the gorge or walk on a few yards to the metal gate, part of the fenceline that once separated the

Ruiz/Alvarado and Johnson/Taylor ranches. Several small paths lead down to the creek for a better view of the waterfall. Any way you go, you can rest or picnic on the peñasquitos—but please don't leave any trash behind.

When you're ready to leave, take the main road back. It's not as secluded, but it will cut about a mile off your round-trip distance.

If you're lucky, as we've been on several occasions, you might see one of the canyon's resident bobcats walking across the road. They look like long-legged housecats, but won't respond to a call of "Here, kitty, kitty." There's an equally good chance of spotting a deer or coyote—Peñasquitos is the last refuge of local wildlife.

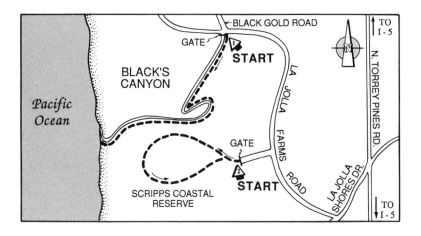

Black's Canyon and Scripps Coastal Reserve

◆

LOCATION:

La Jolla.

Black's Canyon: Take I-5 to La Jolla Village Drive, go west past the University of California (U.C.S.D.) campus to La Jolla Shores Drive; take a left and a quick right to La Jolla Farms Road. The entrance gate is on your left, about 0.5 mile in, opposite Blackgold Road. Unless you're planning a short stay, park at the end of the two-hour parking signs a few hundred yards ahead, and walk back to the gate (TB38:B6).

View from the top of Scripps Coastal Reserve

Scripps Coastal Reserve: Heading back toward La Jolla Shores on La Jolla Farms Road, look on the right for a circular drive and a tall wooden fence with a black metal gate. The sign says "Scripps Coastal Reserve." Park on the street, where you're not on private property (TB44:B1).

HOURS:

Always open.

DESCRIPTION:

At Black's Canyon, a dramatic descent from the million-dollar mesa-top homes of La Jolla Farms leads to one of the county's best and least accessible beaches. Wonderful ocean views framed by steep green slopes greet you at every switchback of this paved vehicle road, which is closed to all cars but those of local residents lucky enough to have access keys.

Strong-legged bicyclers, joggers, and board-toting surfers frequent this route, which is the safest shortcut to celebrated Black's Beach. The southern section of beach is owned by U.C.S.D.; the city-owned section extends up to state-owned Torrey Pines Beach.

Just down the street is Scripps Coastal Reserve, an archaeological site that is part of the University of California's Natural Reserve System, which protects sensitive habitats and endangered plants and animals. There are equally wonderful views here, but no beach access.

Aside from a pay phone at the top of Black's Canyon, there are no facilities.

HISTORY:

The La Jolla Farms area was developed in the late 1940s by William H. Black, a Texas oil millionaire, who bought up 200 acres of the Biological Cliffs Hunting Reserve owned by the Scripps family and located between World War II Camp Callan and the ocean.

Originally, he was going to reserve the land for a few select friends who could afford fine homes and horses. He built Blackgold Stables on Torrey Pines Road to train thoroughbred racehorses and polo ponies; riding trails led from the stables down to the beach.

Ultimately, Black subdivided his property into 1- and 2-acre sites, including stable use and membership in his Bridle Club. In 1967, he died on the golf course at the La Jolla Beach and Tennis Club, and U.C.S.D. acquired the still-unsold 130 acres from his son.

Black's Beach became a popular gathering place for nude sunbathers, and in 1974, the city of San Diego declared it a "swimsuit optional zone." By 1977, they had changed their minds, and the controversial legal status was revoked. For awhile, police issued tickets to under-dressed beachgoers, who began to signal each other with whistles whenever the law was in sight.

Today, a truce prevails, though the Black family, embarrassed by all the to-do, has had its name officially removed from the beach.

BLACK'S CANYON
◆ The Walk
DISTANCE: 1.6 miles round trip. TIME: 30 to 40 minutes.

This beautiful walk has an almost Hawaiian feel to it—if Hawaii had chaparral. On the slopes, you'll see sagebrush, lemonade berry, locoweed, prickly pear, cholla, and barrel cactus. The ravines, recipients of run-off from the homes above, are filled with the New Zealand import, myoporum, a fast-growing evergreen that loves salt air. In spring, look for orange-colored dodder covering the sage and the buckwheat. Picturesquely called devil's sewing thread or witch's hair, this leafless parasite was used by Indians as a cure for black widow spider bites; only the dodder on buckwheat was considered effective. There are signs of funnel spider nearby—their webs have a noticeable funnel at the center. Hidden at the base of its funnel, the spider waits for dinner to drop in.

In early spring, with the blooming of bush sunflower and sea dahlia, the hills are carpeted with yellow flowers. That's when you'll see wild cucumber, radish, and, if you're looking hard, some miner's lettuce and polypody ferns.

But the best feature of this walk, in any season, is its striking vistas of hillsides and sea. About halfway down, you'll start to hear the ocean's roar; till then, only birdsong breaks the silence. Look up now and again to catch a hawk making lazy circles in the sky, or a big black raven.

Down at the bottom, there's a pileup of rocks from recent slides; you may have to pick your way over some of them. It's never a good idea to stay too close to the crumbling sandstone cliffs, but they are impressive, 350 feet high and stretching up the coast all the way to Del Mar.

Once at the beach, you have three choices: go north, go south, or go home. If you're planning a beach walk, check a tidetable before you go; high tides can make parts of the trip rocky and wet.

1. North is where the waves are best, the sandstone formations most varied, and the beach turns "swimsuit optional." You may pass joggers wearing only their running shoes, a nude family frolicking with their dog, or, as we once did, a naked bagpiper playing "The Yellow Rose of Texas."

About a mile in, you'll see a number of tiny people making their way down the cliffs from the gliderport. This narrow, precipitous path is recommended only for the very hardy and sure of foot. The figures on the cliff top look remarkably antlike from here—and they're probably saying the same about you.

When the winds are right, there are hang gliders soaring overhead, one of the added attractions of Black's Beach. Glider planes used to take off from here too, but now they're only allowed on special occasions.

At low tide, you can usually walk all the way to the mouth of the San Dieguito River at the north end of Del Mar, a good 6 miles away. The green patch you see at about 2 miles is the Torrey Pines golf course. Just north of it is Torrey Pines State Reserve, where the cliff colors change from beige sandstone to the green, yellow, and red layers that indicate three different eras and are called, respectively, Delmar, Torrey, and Lindavista formations. The gray-green Delmar Formation is the lowest and oldest, and contains the fossil remains of oysters, clams, and other shellfish that lived in the seas 50 million years ago.

This long stretch of beach is great for picnics, but take your trash with you when you leave. In recent years, litter has been a problem here.

There are only a few trash cans, often filled to overflowing, and garbage collection is sporadic.

2. If you choose to head south along the beach, you'll pass the "mushroom house," a beach house with its own private funicular (cable car) to the mesa top. The Coastal Commission would never allow this kind of construction now, but they've let it stand. It's about 0.5 mile to Dike Rock, one of the few volcanic formations on the coast; at low tide there are tidepools to explore.

Before crossing under the new Scripps Pier, you might want to take the ramp uphill to visit Scripps Aquarium, where marine animals from local waters and Baja's Sea of Cortez are on display. You can continue south along La Jolla Shores Beach, about another mile, stopping off for a drink or a snack on Avenida de la Playa.

3. Whatever you do, remember to save yourself for the trip back. It's a steep walk up from the beach to Blackgold, so take it easy.

SCRIPPS COASTAL RESERVE

◆ The Walk
DISTANCE: 0.7 mile loop. TIME: 20 minutes.

Just off La Jolla Farms, overlooking the sea, is this ancient site inhabited by La Jollans 2000 to 5000 years ago.

Duck under the metal gate and follow the path through what was

Looking toward La Jolla

once an Indian village. Skeletal remains recovered from a dig here were stored in a garage for safekeeping during World War II, but somehow, by the end of the war, they had disappeared. One hopes they found a safe resting place and weren't tossed out with the trash.

As you stroll past wild oats, foxtails, and other grasses, watch the sandy path for snake tracks and gopher holes. You'll see lots of wild radish here in spring, its pastel flowers followed by seed pods that look like small green beans.

In the early part of the century, this was prime lima bean farmland. During World War II, foxholes and gun emplacements were set up to defend San Diego from attack by Japanese submarines.

The mound to your left as you head toward the water is all that's left of an old World War II rifle range. There were two military camps nearby: Camp Matthews, located where U.C.S.D. is today, and Camp Callan, near the present Torrey Pines Golf Course. No subs were ever sighted, but our boys were prepared.

You might want to picnic on the bluffs overlooking the beach, close to some oversized bladderpod and not far from the remains of an old foxhole. The view is lovely, and you won't have to worry about crowds.

Kate O. Sessions Memorial Park

LOCATION:

Pacific Beach. Take I-5 to the Garnet/Balboa exit. Go west to Lamont Street, which becomes Soledad Road. Turn right and continue past Loring, turning right at Park Drive, which leads to the parking area (TB52:B2).

HOURS:

Always open.

DESCRIPTION:

Beautifully located on a hillside with panoramic views out to Mission Bay, this 79-acre city park is really two parks in one: grassy slopes for picnicking, kite-flying, ball-playing, frisbee-tossing, and sunset-watching, and a section of chaparral-covered open space for hiking. The developed area has picnic tables, barbecues, restrooms, and drinking water, as well

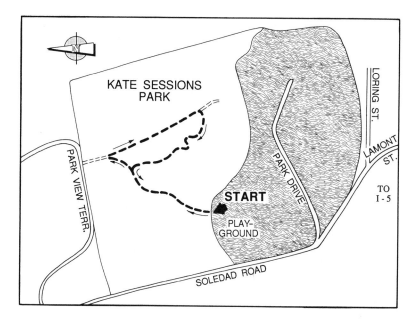

as a 0.75-mile paved walking path. Many of the trees, benches, and drinking fountains have plaques commemorating donors. There's also a playground on the west side of the park, near the trailhead.

HISTORY:

Kate Sessions was an eccentric ex-schoolteacher who started off working in a flower shop and ended up as San Diego's chief gardener.

Known as the Mother of Balboa Park, she was responsible for convincing city fathers to give the old municipal park a new look. By the time of the 1915 Panama-California Exposition, she had helped fill it with hundreds of exotic trees and shrubs, a perfect complement to the romantic Spanish-Moorish architecture of the "temporary" exhibition buildings.

Not only Balboa Park, but all of San Diego benefited from Miss Sessions' beautiful tropical and subtropical plantings. In 1933, after her urging, the city set aside the area on Soledad Road for a park. Originally called Soledad Terrace Park, it was renamed for her in 1957, on the 100th anniversary of her birth. Not far away, at the corner of Garnet and Pico,

Wild cucumber

where her last nursery was located, is a large Brazilian tipuana tree she planted, and a plaque in her memory.

◆ The Walk
DISTANCE: 2 miles round trip. TIME: 1 hour.

Start between the playground and the drinking fountain, at the park's northwest end. Although there are many little trails leading up and down chaparral-covered hillsides, stay on the wider, more traveled path, where many spring flowers can be seen, among them lavender bush mallow, a hollyhock relative. Look for patches of bedstraw, which grows in soft, thick mats and was used by Indians and early settlers to stuff mattresses, pillows, and chair cushions. An Old World variety was said to have lined the manger of the baby Jesus.

The walk takes you down to the bottom of a small canyon where a creek sometimes runs in winter; it's usually dried up by the time the flowers appear. There are trapdoor spiders here, living behind 10-year-old doors, and huge black-and-gold bumblebees, that love the blue-flowered black sage. You'll also see filaree, planted for sheep and cattle to graze on, and tumbleweed, a fall bloomer.

In spring, the wild cucumber shows its spiny green fruit, and the deerweed is covered with tiny yellow blossoms that bees find attractive. The blossoms turn red and start to droop after pollination, signaling the bees to move on to fresher yellow flowers.

The path takes you up to the top of the ridge where you'll find bladderpod, an ill-smelling relative of the capers used in cooking. Uncooked, its bladder-shaped pods are poisonous; early natives found them edible when roasted. You may spot some of the elaborately colored harlequin beetles who call the bladderpod home.

Nearby are dudleya, spring-blooming succulents with long-stemmed red flowers. Dudleya are named for William Russel Dudley, head of the Botany Department at Stanford University around the turn of the century, and forestry editor of the Sierra Club's magazine.

After the spring flowers fade, the slopes here turn brown and dry, waiting for a rejuvenating rain. October brings white-crowned sparrows; their thin whistles are a sure sign that fall is here, even if it's 90 degrees out. Year-round, look for brown towhees, lesser goldfinches, and quail. If you're very lucky, you might even see a fox or a coyote.

As you come out of the canyon, take the main fire road left and uphill to another road heading south across the center of the mesa. This wide trail leads into a narrow one; go right near the first ornamental plants you see, or you'll end up in someone's backyard. Head back along the canyon edge to rejoin the main fire road.

You'll have to go uphill again a few hundred yards before you can make your way back down the canyon to the playground; look for the concrete rubble near the street, marking the easiest descent.

Mission Bay: Once Around the Park

◆

LOCATION:

Pacific Beach/Mission Beach. Take I-5 to Pacific Beach. Go west to Lamont Street, turn left and continue, crossing Crown Point Drive, to the first parking lot (TB52:C5).

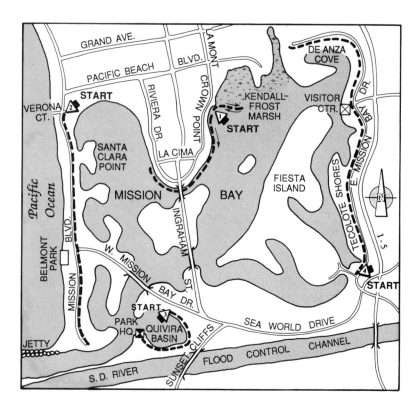

HOURS:

Always open.

DESCRIPTION:

Covering 4600 acres of land and water, Mission Bay is said to be the largest aquatic park in the world. There are grassy picnic areas, playgrounds, sandy beaches, boat launch facilities, and restrooms all around the bay, as well as resort hotels, marinas, a large private campground, and, of course, Sea World. Mission Bay is a popular destination for tourists and residents alike, especially on weekends and during the summer. Try to come at quieter times. The Visitor Information Center, just off I-5 at Clairemont Drive, can give you all the standard information; call 276-8200.

HISTORY:

The area now called Mission Bay was once a broad lagoon where Indians came to hunt waterfowl and gather shellfish. It was deep enough to seem a good port to explorer Sebastian Vizcaino when he arrived in 1602.

Over the next two centuries, things changed. The San Diego River, flowing through on its way to the sea, left the bay choked with sediment, a place of shoals and sandbars known to 19th-century sailors as False Bay. Dikes built to keep San Diego Harbor from suffering the same fate only added to False Bay's problems. Fifty years ago it was a large stagnant pond, often used as a trash dump.

When postwar federal funding enabled the building of a flood control channel, the bay was dredged completely, given a new name, and reborn as one of the beauty spots of San Diego.

THE WALKS

Driving or bike riding and walking, it's possible to circle the bay's nearly 27-mile perimeter in a long afternoon.

◆ Walk 1 Feathers to Fossils: Crown Point Shores to La Cima
DISTANCE: 2 miles round trip. TIME: 45 minutes to 1 hour.

To get some idea of what the area looked like in the old days, start at the Kendall-Frost Marsh Reserve, at the east end of the Crown Point Drive parking lot.

Walk east along the shoreline, passing the fenced area reserved for the endangered least terns, which actually seem to prefer the man-made islands in the bay. About 0.1 mile in, you can sit down on a sand dune and spend a few quiet moments trying to identify some of the 107 bird species that congregate here. It's best to come at high tide, when they're all squeezed up onto the sandbar.

This is a good place to see black skimmers, the black-and-white, orange-legged tropical birds who decided, as other visitors have, that temperate San Diego was a fine spot to settle down and raise their young. In the past 10 years, they've increased their numbers to over 200. They owe their name to their habit of feeding by skimming over the water, dragging their lower bills along the surface to pick up small fish and shellfish.

Other shorebirds you can pick out of the feathered crowd are brown curlews, with their long, downcurving bills, and marbled godwits, also brown, but with shorter upturned bills, as if pointing up to God.

When you're through birdwatching, walk westward, stopping if you like for a picnic on the sand or the grass. You'll be passing under the Ingraham Street bridge and heading toward Sail Bay, popular with weekend sailors.

Just before La Cima Drive and the second set of concrete steps leading up to the street, look for 200,000-year-old sand dollars sticking out from the eroding cliffside. These fossils are similar to the sand dollars found on our beaches today, but, not unexpectedly, a little more worn and fragile.

Unless the tide is high, you can continue walking around Sail Bay, past the Catamaran Hotel, and on to the Bayside Walk.

◆ Walk 2 Bayside Walk: Verona Court to the Jetty

DISTANCE: 4 miles round trip. TIME: 1.5 hours.

Park if you can on Mission Boulevard, or 0.5 mile ahead, at Santa Clara Point, where you can rent boats, take lessons in all kinds of water sports, or just stretch out on the grass. The paved and generally peaceful Bayside Walk crosses West Mission Bay Drive, where you may want to stop in at Belmont Park, on the west side of Mission Boulevard.

In 1925, this was the site of an amusement park built by John D. Spreckels, the millionaire sugar king who owned, among other things, most of Coronado Island, two of San Diego's three newspapers, a water supply company, and the "Impossible Railroad," the SDA&E, connecting San Diego to the East Coast. The park featured a large indoor swimming pool called The Plunge and a roller coaster called The Giant Dipper. The area was reborn as a shopping center in 1988, with The Plunge remodeled and reopened. A state historical landmark, the old wooden roller coaster is slated for restoration and should be back in business sometime in 1990, along with a "coaster museum."

Here, on the ocean side of the street, you can take advantage of the paved beachfront promenade for biking, skating, walking, and people-watching. Head north to Crystal Pier or south to the Jetty, but don't expect to have the path to yourself, especially in warm weather.

Just across from Belmont Park, on the corner of Mission Boulevard and West Mission Bay Drive, is Bonita Cove, whose grassy hill is nice for picnics, kite-flying, or frisbee-tossing. It's another mile along the Bayside Walk to the Jetty, where you can watch boats coming through the channel or continue your walk along the ocean.

Note: Don't even *think* of bringing your car to Mission Boulevard on a sunny weekend afternoon. You'll be stuck in traffic for hours!

◆ Walk 3 Seafood to Seabirds: Quivira Basin

DISTANCE: 2 miles round trip. TIME: 45 minutes to 1 hour.

When you're in the mood for a seafood lunch, a bike or boat rental, a few hours of sportfishing or whalewatching, or just a quiet dockside walk, drive east on West Mission Bay Drive and turn right into the parking lot at Quivira Road. (For determined nondrivers, there are sidewalks and bike lanes along West Mission Bay Drive.)

Stroll past the boat slips and the restaurants and shops of Marina Village to Hospitality Point, headquarters of Mission Bay Park, where you'll find good birdwatching in the flood control channel. Look for

Cliffs at La Cima, Mission Bay

cormorants, pelicans, and, in winter, visiting loons. The oldest living birds on earth, loons have managed to survive even though they can't walk on land and need at least 0.25 mile of water runway to get themselves airborne. You'll see them swimming low in the water, keeping an ancient eye out for fish.

◆ Walk 4 Kites and Windsurfers: East Mission Bay

DISTANCE: 5 miles round trip. TIME: 1.5 to 2 hours.

Last but not least, try a long, leisurely walk from the corner of East Mission Bay and Sea World Drive to De Anza Cove, passing broad grassy areas, the Hilton Hotel, a number of little beaches, and the Visitor Information Center. On weekends, kite enthusiasts gather at Tecolote Shores, filling the air with flying fish, birds, and dragons. Windsurfers like to launch their bright-colored sailboards near the Information Center, and *everybody* seems to like to picnic on this side of the bay.

If you prefer, you can walk north to south, parking at De Anza Cove, and heading toward man-made Fiesta Island, left in its "natural" state, where the annual Over-The-Line Tournament, a wild and crazy kind of three-man (or woman) softball, is held.

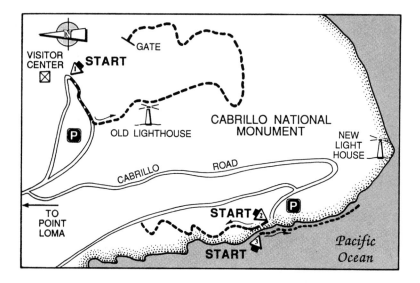

Cabrillo National Monument

◆

LOCATION:

Point Loma. Take I-5 to Rosecrans and go west. At Cañon, turn right; continue to Catalina Boulevard and turn left. Catalina soon becomes Cabrillo Memorial Drive. Pass through Fort Rosecrans National Cemetery and continue on to the end of the point (TB64:B6).

HOURS:

9:00 a.m. to sunset. $3.00 parking fee at visitor's center. Tidepool Area, 9:00 a.m. to 4:30 p.m.; no fee.

DESCRIPTION:

San Diego's only national monument, Cabrillo is a beautiful place indeed, with sweeping views of San Diego Bay and the Pacific Ocean. There are tidepools to explore, an old lighthouse to visit, and several scenic nature trails to follow. The visitor's center has a small historical museum, daily talks, slide shows and films, and an excellent bookshop. You can picnic and bay-watch between the visitor's center and the parking lot, or at tables in the grove between the lot and the old lighthouse. Snack and drink machines and, of course, restrooms can be found at the visitor's center.

Cabrillo offers ranger-led nature, tidepool, and military history walks, and in winter, special talks and films on the gray whale migration. Check the bulletin board outside the auditorium, or call 557-5450 for schedules.

HISTORY:

Long before Cabrillo's time, Diegueño Indians lived on Point Loma. But the monument is named for the Portuguese navigator who had served under Cortez in Mexico and was hoping to discover the coast of New Spain and, perhaps, a shortcut from the Pacific to the Atlantic Ocean.

In June 1542, Juan Rodriquez Cabrillo sailed northward under the Spanish flag, arriving at San Diego Bay on September 28. He went ashore near Ballast Point, naming the area San Miguel in honor of Saint Michael, whose feast day it was. Six days later, he sailed away, discovered Los Angeles, and broke a leg going ashore at the Channel Islands. Gangrene set in, and within a few months, he was dead.

The old Point Loma Lighthouse, built in 1854, was in operation until 1891, when it was replaced by the lighthouse near the tidepools. Over 450 feet above sea level, it was so high that its light was often obscured by fog and low clouds. During World War II, when Point Loma was the backbone of a coastal defense system, it was used as a military radio station.

In 1913, the lighthouse and the quarter acre of land around it were declared a national monument, commemorating Europe's discovery of the West Coast. Since then, the park has grown to 144 acres, and is, after the Statue of Liberty, the second most visited national monument in the U.S.

◆ Walk 1 Bayside Trail

DISTANCE: 3 miles round trip. TIME: 1.5 hours.

Before starting out, consider picking up a trail guide at the visitor's center, where our walk begins. It's only 25 cents and full of information on plants, Indian lore, and history. Then take the road heading south toward the old lighthouse. At about 0.2 mile you'll notice a paved service road leading downhill to your left; stay on the marked shoulder for another 0.3 mile and take the next road on the left. This is the actual start of the Bayside Trail.

Once a military patrol road, the trail winds down the eastern slope of Point Loma with great views all the way. During World War II, Point

Loma was honeycombed with bunkers, cannons, and mortars to protect the harbor from Japanese attack; you'll see some of the remains along the trail.

There are occasional benches to rest on as you make the 300-foot descent, and, more importantly, as you climb back up. Take your time and enjoy the view; these chaparral-covered slopes will give you an idea of what San Diego looked like when Cabrillo came, with the notable exception of the eucalyptus trees, which didn't get here until the late 1800s.

In spring, the hillsides are covered with yellow bush sunflower, sometimes called brown-eyed susan, and red flashes of monkey flower and Indian paintbrush.

To the south, you'll see a constant parade of naval vessels, pleasure craft, fishing boats, and ocean liners moving in and out of the harbor. On clear days, you can see Mexico's Coronado Islands and some of the more elegant homes of Tijuana's Las Playas section. Often, there are navy jets leaving or landing on North Island; a display outside the visitor's center will help you identify planes and ships, if you're so inclined.

At #13, there are traces of a 50-million-year-old streambed that flowed into the sea when water still covered the land. The rounded "plug" of grayish mudstone is even older than the surrounding yellow sandstone—about 2 million years older. A few yards below is a break in the rock that indicates an earthquake fault.

At low tide, watch for pelicans, cormorants, and, sometimes, sea lions basking on the rocks of the jetty. Continuing on, you'll see San Diego's skyline and the mountains beyond. At the trail's end, about 1 mile from the trailhead, you can look ahead to Ballast Point, the slim finger of land where Cabrillo landed. Its name comes from its use as a ballast dump for 19th-century sailing ships, which used rocks, sand, and dirt to balance the weight of their cargo. Many of the paving stones for San Diego's streets came from here, as did many of the seeds of introduced plants like hottentot fig, tree tobacco, and wild radish, which came with the ballast and stayed on to sprout and reproduce wherever they ended up.

Today, at Ballast Point, you can still see ships, but more modern ones—the navy's nuclear-powered submarines.

Turn around at the fence and follow the trail back up to the visitor's center. If you're still in the mood, try another walk.

◆ Walk 2 Seaside Trail

DISTANCE: 2 miles round trip. TIME: 45 minutes.

Just before you come to the main parking area, there's a paved road on your right that leads downhill to the working lighthouse and the Point Loma sewage treatment plant. To your left at the bottom is a small parking lot. From it, you can pick up one of the trails that meander around the

Juan Rodriguez Cabrillo

Old lighthouse at Cabrillo National Monument

bluffs on the west side of Point Loma, overlooking the Pacific Ocean.

Start at the north side of the lot. Take the steps down to the bottom, then curve right around the gully and look for the trail heading uphill; the trail to your left leads down to the tidepools. Here on the cliff's edge, you can have good views of the sea and the occasional cormorant or gull flying by. Up here, you're higher than they are!

At about 0.5 mile, the trail meets the road; avoid it and go downhill into the lemonade berry and acacia. Take the lowest trail, heading seaward, walking along the cliff's edge.

In spring, look for poppies, deerweed, lupines, and other familiar wildflowers, dwarfed, as are all the plants on this side, by the constant salt spray and sea breezes. At about 0.7 mile, you'll see the rare Shaw's agave, a short, broad succulent that looks like the top of a large pineapple. Soon you'll start heading up toward the road; a good turnaround point is the sign prohibiting the taking of specimens, about 1 mile from the parking lot.

◆ Walk 3 Tidepool Walk
DISTANCE: 1 mile round trip. TIME: 1 to 2 hours.

On low tide days, especially in fall and winter, don't miss Cabrillo's fine tidepools (see Exploring Tidepools, page 189). Go out on a descending tide and be prepared to get your feet wet; the best finds are around the point, about 0.5 mile in. You'll have to do some wading to get there. Remember: Look but don't take, and if you've never been tidepooling before, try to arrange your visit to coincide with one of the ranger-led walks.

Tijuana River Valley

LOCATION:

Imperial Beach.
Tijuana River National Estuarine Reserve
Take I-5 south to Coronado Avenue in Imperial Beach. Go west. Coronado Avenue becomes Imperial Beach Boulevard at 13th Street (TB70Z:F5).

For Walk 1: Turn left at the unobtrusive church, St. Mary's by the Sea, on the corner of 5th Street. Drive south a few blocks and park near Iris Street.

For Walk 2: Turn left on 4th Street and right on Caspian Way. Park on Caspian or 3rd Street.

For Walk 3: Turn left on Seacoast Drive, continue to the end, and park.

Border Field State Park
For Walks 4 and 5: Take I-5 south to the Coronado Avenue exit. Cross Coronado and continue south on Hollister. At Monument Road turn right, go to the end and park by the entry booth. For picnic area or restrooms, drive on to the regular parking areas about 0.5 mile ahead (TB73:A3).

HOURS:

Tijuana River National Estuarine Reserve is always open except the Tidal Creek side of Seacoast Drive, which is closed during least tern nesting, April 15 to September 15. Visitor's center, call 575-3613 for hours. Border Field State Park: Summer, 8:30 a.m. to 7:00 p.m.; $4.00 parking fee. Winter, 9:30 a.m. to 5:00 p.m.; no fee.

DESCRIPTION:

Although known officially, since 1982, as the Tijuana River National Estuarine Reserve, old timers still call it the Slough. Southern California's largest remaining estuary and wetland, it covers about 2500 acres of wet-

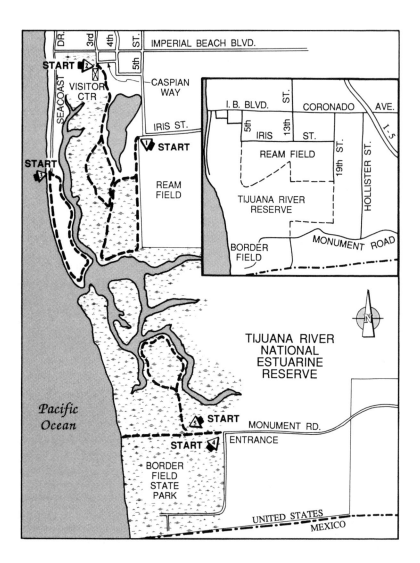

land and upland habitats, including the Tijuana Slough National Wildlife Refuge and Border Field State Park.

Most of the water that drains into the Tijuana River comes from Mexico, but the entire estuary is within U.S. borders. Over 245 species of birds frequent the reserve, finding plenty of shellfish, worms, and fish for food. Several endangered species—the least tern, brown pelican, savannah sparrow, least Bell's vireo, clapper rail, and peregrine falcon—can be found here. Since flooding is common, the days just after a rainstorm are not a good time to come. The only facilities are the picnic tables, barbecues, and restrooms at Border Field State Park, and restrooms at the new visitor's center.

HISTORY:

On very old maps this area was known as the Oneonta Slough. Its fertile river valley was the site of a colony of cooperative farmers founded by utopian idealist William E. Symthe near what is now San Ysidro. Calling themselves "Little Landers," 129 families, each with a little land of their own, raised poultry, goats, and produce. They had their own school, library, and community center, and prospered until early 1916, when the flood attributed to rainmaker Charles Hatfield covered their fields with tons of mud and sand (see Lake Morena Park, p. 172). By 1918, the colony had disbanded.

Later, parts of the river valley became a sewage dump. During World War II, military installations were built to protect the coast from enemy attack. A small railroad dragged targets out across the dunes for machine gun practice. Ream Field, named for the army's first flight surgeon, Major William Roy Ream, is still used by naval helicopters to practice landings and air-sea rescues.

TIJUANA RIVER NATIONAL ESTUARINE RESERVE

◆ Walk 1   5th and Iris

DISTANCE: 2.5 miles round trip. TIME: 1.5 hours.

This is the boundary of the reserve and Ream Field, where on weekdays, you can see—and hear—more helicopters than anywhere outside of "Apocalypse Now."

Enter at the "National Reserve" sign, following the wide path along the boundary fence. At about 0.75 mile, you can follow the higher and dryer path or cross the log barrier and go down a few hundred feet to the narrower path along the river's edge. Either path heads west toward the river mouth, leading into great birdwatching territory. There are usually dozens of terns, gulls, sandpipers, egrets, ducks, and pelicans down by the river.

In the marshy lowlands, you'll see pickleweed, alkali heath, and taller stands of cordgrass, all typical of our salt marshes. In the mudflats, at low tide, there are cockles, fiddler crabs, and horn snails, whose shells look like tiny cornucopias. The tidal creeks are home to a number of small fish, like silvery top smelt and anchovies, much loved by terns and pelicans. Larger halibut and croaker come here to spawn.

Above the dryer uplands, covered with buckwheat, sagebrush, and lemonade berry, look for marsh hawks, also called harriers, easily identified by their white rump spots.

From the river mouth, take the same path back or make a circle by following the wide trail that angles across the marsh. This will take you past several ponds once used for sand and gravel mining, now home to many kinds of waterbirds, including the rare little blue heron. After about 1.5 miles, you'll connect up with the wide fenceside path bordering Ream Field.

◆ Walk 2 Caspian and 3rd

DISTANCE: 2 miles round trip. TIME: 1 hour.

By the end of 1989, there'll be a visitor's center here, run by the U.S. Department of Fish and Wildlife, with interactive exhibits on wetlands wildlife and salt marsh ecology and special classes for children and adults. Ranger-led walks are currently being held on the first two Saturdays of every month. For details, call 237-6766.

The trail leads out from the visitor's center into the marsh, connecting up with the trails mentioned in Walk 1, making it possible to walk all the way to the river mouth.

On the right side of the path is a cordgrass meadow that looks like an overgrown lawn. Thriving in the tidal ebb and flow, cordgrass is the preferred habitat of endangered clapper rails, secretive marsh birds that use the grass to hide in and to construct their nests. In 1983, storms pushed the barrier sand dunes into the tidal creeks, preventing salt water from coming in, and killing the cordgrass. Predictably, the clapper rails disappeared. Now many areas of the estuary are closed while cordgrass is reintroduced, in hope that the hand-clapping sound of the clapper rail will soon be heard again.

◆ Walk 3 Seacoast Drive

DISTANCE: 2 miles round trip. TIME: 1 hour.

Start at the metal gate at the end of the street and walk south along the channel, past the summer nesting grounds of the endangered least terns. Thousands of these small birds used to nest in San Diego County, scraping shallow nests in the sand in June and July and standing over the eggs to shade them and keep them cool. As sunbathers increasingly spread out over the beaches, the numbers of least terns declined. Today, there are probably only 1200 pairs left in all Southern California. From mid-April to mid-September the area along the tidal creek is closed to human traffic, so the least terns can breed in peace; the beach side of the dunes is open year-round. Rare snowy plovers, tiny relatives of killdeer, also make their shallow nests in the dunes in summer.

Speaking of things endangered, consider the dunes themselves,

Cordgrass, Tijuana River Valley. Photo by Julie Bubar

which protect the estuary's fragile ecosystem. Dune-growing plants can survive nowhere else. Purple sand verbena, pink sea rocket—related to wild radish—and yellow dune primrose are all low-growing plants that stabilize the sand and provide food and shelter for burrowing insects and the California legless lizard, which looks like a small pale snake. San Diego used to have sand dunes along all of its low-lying beaches; development has bulldozed most of them away.

After the storms of 1983, the dunes here were pushed into the river channel, closing the mouth of the river. The sand was dredged out, and the dunes were rebuilt and replanted; they are now off-limits to walkers.

We like to walk south along the tidal creek, and return along the beach. It's usually empty, and you can look out toward the Coronado Islands, 12 miles offshore. Discovered in 1602 by Sebastian Vizcaino, these islands are now a Mexican wildlife preserve and closed to visitors.

BORDER FIELD STATE PARK

Built in the shadow of Tijuana's Bullring by the Sea, this 400-acre state park stands at the southwestern corner of the United States. Straddling the border is a pyramid-shaped monument marking the international boundary set here in 1848, after the Treaty of Guadalupe Hidalgo made California American territory.

In 1974, Pat Nixon cut the ribbon at the park's dedication ceremony and immediately crossed the border to shake hands with all the Mexican citizens who were watching the goings-on, much to the dismay of the Secret Service. Today, the Border Patrol keeps a wary eye on the monument picnic area and the unfenced beach below. You can cross over into Mexico there, but you may not be able to return; this is not a legal border crossing.

Take a short paved walk around the perimeter of the picnic area and admire the view of the ocean and the hills of Tijuana. Display panels in both English and Spanish describe the estuary and its human and natural history.

The beach, reached from the lower parking lot, is never crowded. Nice as it looks, though, we don't recommend swimming here. All too often, sewage washes up from Mexico. When this happens, the park's main road may be closed; call 435-5184 to check conditions before starting out.

This is the only beach in the county where horseback riding is allowed; rental horses are available at stables along Hollister Street or Monument Road. Walking or riding, from the lower parking lot, it's just over 2 miles to the mouth of the Tijuana River.

Both walks here begin at the wide equestrian trail west of the entry booth. Riders may come along at a gallop—give them the right of way. Like all wetland areas, these can be too wet to walk after heavy rainfall or extremely high tides.

◆ Walk 4 Beach Trail

DISTANCE: 1.5 miles round trip. TIME: 30 to 45 minutes.

The equestrian trail leads through masses of tumbleweed and true iceplant, whose small white flowers are followed by magenta seed pods that turn brown in winter. After rain, the succulent leaves begin to grow. Bright green, they may get as big as your hand, but as the flowers start to bloom, they gradually shrink away. Iceplant does have a sort of frosty look, but on closer inspection, you can see that buds and leaves are actually covered with tiny liquid-filled beadlets—the plant's way of storing moisture.

At about 0.3 mile, you can pick up the hiking trail to your right (see Walk 5) or continue for another 0.5 mile to the beach. Just before the beach, you'll cross a low cement "bridge" over usually shallow water where shorebirds and ducks come to feed. Next there's a wooden bridge across the revegetated sand dunes—the only approved dune crossing. Then you're at the beach, with a 360-degree view from Point Loma to Tijuana, including the Coronado Islands. You can beach-walk south to the border or north to the river mouth, or head back to pick up Walk 5.

◆ Walk 5 Tidal Creek Loop

DISTANCE: 2 miles round trip. TIME: 45 minutes to 1 hour.

From the parking lot, follow the equestrian trail 0.3 mile and turn right. This side trail leads off through the haplopappus, more commonly called goldenbush, and past a not-so-old cement foundation; until 1970, there was military housing here.

This broad flat expanse is a good place to see jackrabbits and brush bunnies. Jackrabbits are the ones with the really large ears; brush bunnies have the white cotton tails.

Cross a mudflat and continue on through boxthorn and clumps of pickleweed, following a tidal creek where willets, dowitchers, curlews, sandpipers, and ducks can be seen. At about a mile, you move from uplands to lowlands—a difference of just a few feet in elevation, but enough for the boxthorn to give way to acres of pickleweed—green in summer, magenta in fall, red-tipped in winter. Look also for sea lavender; with its delicate branches and tiny white flowers, it looks something like baby's breath. The large red-tinged leaves at the base of the plant may be covered with crystals of salt. Coastal Indians used to brush the salt off the leaves, and use it to season their food.

Turn left at the "No Horses" sign and continue on toward the dunes. You'll get a victim's-eye view of the Ream Field helicopters, circling like motorized marsh hawks. The path narrows through the pickleweed, but press on to the channel at about 1.3 miles, where you can see black-and-white avocets, and, sometimes, a little blue heron.

From here, take the path heading southward toward the hills of Tijuana. It widens to an old vehicle road, recrosses the mudflat, and finally rejoins the equestrian trail where we left it.

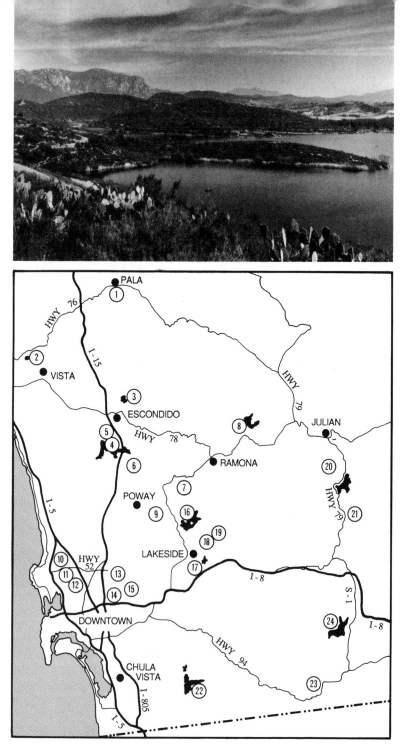

INLAND
SAN DIEGO

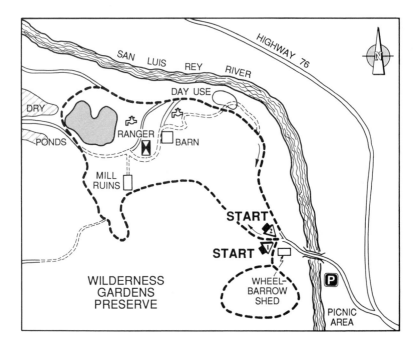

Wilderness Gardens Preserve

◆

LOCATION:

Pala. Take I-15 north to Highway 76. Go east 10 miles to the entrance, on the right about 1 mile past Agua Tibia Ranch, near a sign that says "Rancho Pecaro" (TB400:D3).

HOURS:

9:30 a.m. to 5:00 p.m. Open Friday through Monday. Closed during August. $1.00 parking fee. *Note:* The preserve was temporarily closed in 1992 until repairs were completed. Check before going there.

DESCRIPTION:

This 584-acre county park of mixed woodlands and chaparral is one of our favorite inland destinations. It's a lovely, uncrowded place to walk, fish, or picnic. It's also a good place to camp, but only organized groups are allowed. Facilities are basic—well water, outhouses, and picnic tables (one with handicapped access). Main attractions are the fishing pond and the flowers that bloom in the spring, which include hundreds of camellias among the less exotic vegetation. For further information, call County Parks, 565-3600.

HISTORY:

For centuries before the Spanish came, the area around Pala was an Indian campground; Pala Peak was said to be a sacred spot. In the early 1800s, the padres set up a chapel at Pala as an adjunct to the San Luis Rey Mission, and the land nearby was planted with grain, and also with cotton, to clothe the Indian converts.

Indian reservations were established in the area in the 1870s, despite the protests of local Anglos who thought the land was too good to give away to Indians.

Pala is an Indian word for "water," and the San Luis Rey River still runs through here year-round. In the 1880s, a local miller, M. M. Sickler, diverted the river and used it to power his grist mill. Many Indians, believing that spirits living in the water controlled its flow, were convinced that Sickler had captured one of them and locked him inside the turbine; it was the spirit's desperate struggle to escape that made the mill wheel keep turning.

In the 1950s, Los Angeles publisher Manchester Boddy, founder of Descanso Gardens in La Cañada, bought the acreage for a retirement retreat and named it Wilderness Gardens. He planted 100,000 of his beloved camellias here, and put in five ponds to irrigate them. At present, only one of the ponds has water in it, and only a few hundred camellias remain, but they still put on an impressive springtime display.

After Boddy's death in 1967, the gardens were abandoned and threatened with development. Rescued by Small Wilderness Area Preserves (SWAP), a statewide organization, the preserve was opened to the public as a walk-in facility in 1983.

THE WALKS

Whether you want a short walk or a long one, start at the parking lot. There's a kiosk near the entrance, with a large park map; occasionally, you'll find information brochures here.

Walk in the entrance, where the grapevines twine; wild grapes are smaller than blueberries, and practically all seed. Cross the small bridge over the usually docile river. Once the San Luis Rey River had power enough to carve out the canyon we're walking through, but that was before it was dammed at Lake Henshaw. Now, you can find crayfish here, those miniature lobsters that live only in slow-moving fresh water.

San Luis Rey River

Continue along into the trees—cottonwoods, live oaks, sycamores, and willows—all typical streamside dwellers. You'll notice a lot of poison oak growing in the park; try to notice it from a distance, and don't be attracted by its fall color, as one of our TV newspersons was several years ago, posing for the cameras with a big bouquet of it in her arms.

A few hundred yards from the entrance is a wheelbarrow shed, where campers can load up their gear to trundle over to their sites. Both walks begin here, taking the Upper Meadow Trail to the left.

◆ Walk 1 The Sensory Trail

DISTANCE: 0.3 mile round trip. TIME: 15 minutes.

This is soon to be a kind of sensory parcourse, wheelchair accessible, with signs in Braille for blind visitors and suggested sense-sharpening exercises for others. So far, there are only empty signposts, and none of what one park volunteer here called "verbage," but things should be completed by the end of 1989.

Go left at the fork and follow the unmarked posts through the coast live oaks, with prickly pear growing among them. In spring, there's lots of deerweed growing here, with more bees than deer attracted to its small yellow and red flowers.

Tall oaks from little acorns grow, as you can tell along the trail, where you can see them in various stages of development. You can sit on a fallen tree trunk and study the process, and the holes in the bark made by boring insects, which are actually rather interesting insect drillers, helping the dead tree to decompose and enrich the soil.

Bear left at the fork, passing a few small cottonwoods, which will doubtless be big cottonwoods a few years down the road. As you amble on, listen to the wind rustle through the twinkling cottonwood leaves, making a sound like raindrops.

There's another insect phenomenon to watch for: ant-lion pits. At the bottom of each of these small, upside-down volcanoes is an ant-lion larva, or "doodle-bug," waiting for an insect lunch to drop in. The mature ant-lion is more like a dragonfly, and flies off in search of its food.

After about 0.1 mile, bear right; you'll see Whipple's yucca and, on your right, a fine specimen of tall, pale Great Basin sagebrush, grayer and larger-leafed than the coastal variety, surrounded by buckwheat.

There are occasional benches where you can sit and admire the many shades of green and, in spring, the colors of purple lupine and golden yarrow.

At the trail's end, head back to the "Upper Meadows Trail" sign and the wheelbarrow shed, or turn left at the trail guide box and pick up Walk 2.

◆ Walk 2 Upper Meadows Trail

DISTANCE: 2.5 miles round trip. TIME 1.5 to 2 hours.

From the wheelbarrow shed, follow the trail sign and bear right at the trail guide box. In fall, look for acorns on the ground; the slim pointy ones are live oaks, or will be some day.

Listen for acorn woodpeckers; they sound like rusty bedsprings, if you're old enough to remember what that sounds like. Look for holly-leaf cherry, with its notched leaves and dark brown summer fruits that are more pit than cherry. Its Latin name is *Prunus ilicifolia,* which sounds more like a prune or a plum; Indians called it Islay, and ate it.

You'll see plenty of coyote droppings as you walk along, but it's unlikely that you'll see the generally nocturnal coyotes; keep an eye out for the usual lizards, squirrels, and quail.

At about 0.3 mile, there's a toyon, or California holly, with narrower leaves than the holly-leaf cherry, and yellow berries that start forming in summer, turning to bright red by late October. Just ahead is a large clump of yellow broom, a mass of color when it blooms in early fall, and prettier than the more common coastal variety.

At about 0.5 mile, bypassing the "Private" sign that leads to the ranger's residence, you start to climb uphill. This is usually a good place to listen for the "voice of the chaparral," the wrentit, singing in the scrub higher up.

As you climb, notice the green woodland ferns on the hillsides; even in the middle of summer, there's a cool, woodsy feeling here. You'll soon find yourself walking along the ridge overlooking the ranger residence area, and then looking out across the valley to the mountains, at the foot of which is yet another sand and gravel company, busily grinding up the terrain to make new foundations. Closer at hand, just below you, is a corner of the stone mill that Sickler built 100 years ago.

The trail continues to climb, with wooden steps to help you. There's a short section—only about 25 feet—where you might appreciate a walking stick; you'll certainly want good treads on your shoes.

Then you're at the top of the mesa, with a 360-degree view. You can look down on one of the ponds put in by publisher Boddy to irrigate his camellias. It's the only one that's currently full of water and visited by casual anglers fishing for catfish, bluegill, and bass.

Circle around a dry pond and head down to the wet one. Notice that, up here, you're back in chaparral country, where it's dryer and hotter. The streamside vegetation is down below, near the river.

Tiptoe through the buckwheat, and past a meadow. In fall, everything here looks reddish—buckwheat, sumac flowers, soil, rocks. After all that restful green, it's strange to be walking through the buckwheat's red glare.

At about a mile, you start descending again. Cross a log footbridge and come face to face with a good-sized toyon. If you're ready for more climbing, follow the sign just ahead to the Upper Meadows and Pala Peak; it's about another mile, and you'd do well to carry some water along.

We head down to the ponds and tent sites, back to the woodlands. In winter, there could be water running alongside the trail; in spring, the area is covered with wild cucumber, hairy-flowered clematis vines, and scarlet heart-leaf penstemon.

Just over a mile, there's a dead oak trunk, still standing, pocked with the storage holes of acorn woodpeckers, who usually prefer the softer wood of sycamores.

At about 1.3 miles, you come out at the dirt road that circles the fishing pond. Straight ahead is a willow-shaded, pondside picnic table, if you're ready for lunch. If you're not picnicking, go west, heading around the pond and crossing an earthen dam.

You'll see grapes, willows, mulefat, and horehound fringing the water and cattails in it. You can stop and fish, if you've got a license, or dangle your feet in the water; Wilderness Gardens is no place to rush through, and you'll probably have it all to yourself, especially on weekdays.

Leave the high road at 1.7 miles, just past campsite #3, and take the stone steps down to the dirt vehicle road. Just ahead, past the eucalyptus branch arching over the road, is a crossroads; there's drinking water and an outhouse to your right, near the rusty remains of Boddy's old greenhouse. If you're thirsty, be sure to let the water run before you drink it; otherwise, it will taste strongly of hose or pipe.

A short detour along this road will take you to a fire ring and, left of that, a trail leading to the old stone mill and rusted waterwheel. If you're not thirsty, or interested in water wheels, stay on the main road.

In spring, you might want to try the small trail that starts halfway between the water fountain and the barn. It winds through the camellias, and crosses the main road to the day use area. Look for crayfish in the shallow pools, but be sure to keep an eye out for poison oak. The shady path soon joins the road again, and you're on your way back to the parking lot.

Guajome Regional Park

◆

LOCATION:

Vista. Take I-5 north to Mission Avenue (Highway 76), and go east about 7 miles.

For Walk 1: Turn right at Guajome Lake Road, then right to the park's main entrance (TB7:F6).

For Walk 2: Turn right at North Santa Fe Avenue, then left to the park's lower entrance (TB10:F1).

HOURS:

8:30 a.m. to sunset. $1.00 parking fee.

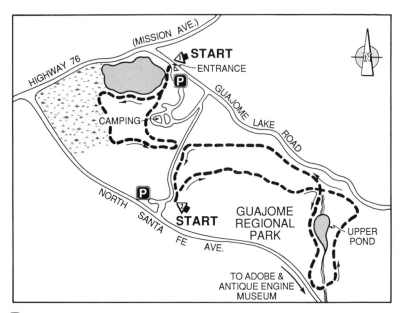

DESCRIPTION:

An attractive 569-acre county park in a part of the county that isn't as rural as it used to be, Guajome is still a good spot to picnic, walk, or camp. Fishermen enjoy the spring-fed, man-made lakes, and the marshy habitats are popular with birds and birdwatchers. There are a number of picnic tables and barbecues, a playground, and a small camping area. For reservations, call County Parks, 565-3600. You can also visit the historic adobe or the Antique Steam and Gas Engine Museum nearby (see By the Way..., p. 95).

HISTORY:

The Indians who inhabited the area around Guajome were called Luiseños by the padres after the building of San Luis Rey Mission in 1798. The land was used for grazing and growing grain until the missions were secularized nearly half a century later. Guajome, an Indian word for "home of the frog," was one of the few land grants actually assigned to Indians—two brothers who soon sold all 2200 acres for $500 to an L.A. merchant, Abel Stearns. He gave it as a wedding present to his young sister-in-law, Ysadora Bandini, and her new husband, Cave Couts.

Couts, a Tennessean who graduated from West Point with Ulysses S. Grant, was an army colonel and a kind of 19th-century "good ole boy." Transferred to San Diego, he stayed at the home of the wealthy Don Juan

Bandini, went into business with him, and married his beautiful daughter in 1851.

With the help of 300 Luiseños, the 20-room adobe ranch house was built, landscaped, and fortified against attack by less tractable Indians. Charged with murder more than once, but always acquitted, Couts probably treated his workers much as he had been used to treating Negro slaves in the South.

He and his wife raised ten children, of whom two died and are said to be buried under the large aloe tree to the left of the chapel door. The Coutses had hundreds of sheep and cattle and were known for their expansive hospitality. Some guests posed special problems. U. S. Grant was asked to leave when he rode his horse into the dining room, and Helen Hunt Jackson, author of *Ramona,* the Indians' *Uncle Tom's Cabin,* tried to stir up an Indian revolt on the property and had to be locked in her room.

After Couts died, his son remodeled the house, married a niece of Mark Twain, and continued the tradition of hospitality. The guests kept on coming, even after the marriage ended. Until his death in 1943, Cave Couts, Jr., liked to be known as the "last of the Dons."

His common-law son lived here until the property was condemned. The county paid him a million dollars for the house and the 165 acres of surrounding land. The adobe was declared a national monument, and the park was opened to the public in 1973.

◆ Walk 1 The Nature Trail
DISTANCE: 2 miles round trip. TIME: 1 hour.

Park opposite the restrooms and follow the paved walkway around, past the playground and picnic areas. Pepper trees and newly planted sycamores line the path, and there's usually a whole lot of quackin' going on down by the water—you may want to bring along some bread to feed the ducks and geese that congregate here. These are a motley crew, offspring of unwanted domestic ducks and wild mallards, and are always hungry.

Where the pavement ends, near the information kiosk, turn left and follow the lakeside path through rows of tall casuarinas, pine-like trees imported from Australia. The straight rows of holes in the trunks are made by red-breasted sapsuckers, who make daily visits to the holes to eat the insects that have been attracted to the sap and trapped there.

At about 0.25 mile, take the right-hand path past the cattails and tules alongside the water. Tules, by the way, is pronounced "too-lees," not "tools." "Out in the tules" is an old local expression for out in the sticks, but recent development has caught up with most of our tules.

In late spring, look for marsh mallows here—not the toastable ones, but a kind of low-growing hollyhock. In winter, after rain, the trail here can get pretty muddy—this is real adobe underfoot. In hot weather, the ground is as parched and cracked as dry clay, which is exactly what it is.

Soon you'll reach the nature trail, which, as is often our habit, we prefer to take backwards. Start at marker #15, a large clump of mallow, tules, and bristly ox-tongue, whose leaves look something like their name but whose flowers look more like dandelions.

Bear right at #15, then, almost immediately, left at #14—some prickly pear cacti. As you cross the willow-shaded bridge, see if you can spot any tadpoles in the water. Remember Guajome means "home of the frog;" you may see some full-grown bullfrogs or bright green California tree frogs here, especially in summer.

After the bridge, turn left. There are clumps of mistletoe in the black willows here, and crested phainopeplas in the mistletoe, especially when the autumn berries start appearing. Phainopeplas, also called silky flycatchers, look like black cardinals—at least the males do. The females and young are gray, but all have white wing patches, visible when flying, and red eyes.

In spring, the maturing seed pods of the black willows look like fluffed-out cotton balls. Sometimes there's so much fluff hanging from the branches it seems almost like snow (remember snow?). You can feel the tiny seeds inside each cottony wad. If you have hay fever, just walk on by; this stuff can make you sneeze.

Soon you'll have to cross over a fallen tree. Look for celery growing just underneath—it has leaves like Italian parsley and tiny white spring flowers. If you're not sure it's celery, squeeze a stalk between your fingers and see if it smells like the store-bought stuff.

There are occasional tree trunks and branches crossing the path from here on, so you'll have to do a bit of ducking and dodging. At #11, there are stinging nettles, with large, long-stemmed notched leaves—don't try squeezing them. Every part of these plants is covered with stinging hairs that contain the same formic acid found in ants. In the old days, Indians beat rheumatism sufferers with nettle switches to try to ease their pain; it sounds a little like trading a headache for an upset stomach. We know a woman who once answered a call of nature in a clump of nettles and was truly sorry for hours afterwards. Some people say you can boil the leaves, and eat them like spinach. We've never felt like trying.

Duck down again up ahead, but don't lift your head too soon; there are two trunks to clear. If it weren't for the unmistakable sounds of traffic nearby, you'd feel as if you were in the middle of a forest.

As you cross the next wooden bridge, listen for a "kek-kek-kek-kek" in the tules, which means there's a Virginia rail nearby. Grayish-brown, with an orange bill, the Virginia rail is a secretive bird; you'd have to be pretty sharp to spot one. You're more likely to see blackbirds—red winged, tri-colored, and yellow-headed ones—sometimes whole flocks of

Upper Pond, Guajome. Photo by Barbara Moore

them out after flying insects.

There's more celery just past #8; then the trail forks left toward the camping area. Unless you're in a hurry to get back, keep to the right and on the nature trail. Up ahead, shaded by willows, is a clump of yerba mansa, which blooms in May and June. Its large white "petals" are really leaves; the yellow cone-shaped centers are the actual flowers. The name in Spanish means "gentle or tame herb;" it's called the "herb of the tame Indian" because Mission Indians used it so often as a general painkiller and for poultices.

Duck again and go on. Ahead on the left is #3, a narrow-leafed willow. Farther along on the right is another #3, the more common black willow; a non-native fan palm has staked out a nice shady spot here. To complete your comparative willow study, check out #1, the arroyo willow. Tall as it is, it's not considered a tree, since it has more than one trunk.

You're now at the main service road. To get back to where you started, bear left, then left again. Walk uphill, keeping the campground to your right. At the crossroads there, head downhill and back through the casuarinas to the parking lot.

◆ Walk 2 The Back-to-Nature Trail
DISTANCE: 3.5 miles round trip. TIME: 1.5 to 2 hours.

This horse trail can get hot in summer, but we love it, since it gives a real sense of the way things used to be. Start at the park's alternate entrance on North Santa Fe, taking the main service road just south of the parking spaces and walking in a few feet to pick up the equestrian trail. Head right toward the houses, alongside a marshy meadow. The fennel forest here attracts black-and-yellow butterflies called anise swallowtails. They lay their eggs on the fennel, which becomes a food supply for the voracious black-and-yellow-striped green caterpillars. While fennel—or anise—is their food of choice, these caterpillars will eat their way through anything in the carrot family.

Despite the occasional houses on the hillsides, you still get a wonderful rural feeling here—so far. Look for hawks and kites, as well as ring-necked pheasants, probably descendants of an exotic bird farm once located nearby. These Asian imports are some of the most colorful birds in San Diego; their bodies and long tail feathers are iridescent bronze, and their green heads are set off by red eye patches and white neck rings.

At about 0.6 mile, in the rock outcropping on your right, you can see ferns, mosses, and lichens after the first winter rains. As you continue on, you'll pass several elderberry trees, whose purple fruit has long been a favorite of home winemakers.

Turn right at the fork in the trail at 0.75 mile, heading uphill through coastal sage scrub. After a few hundred feet, there's a short side trail to your left leading to a shady glade where you can sit on a rock secluded from the world, surrounded by hemlock, elderberry, willows, and poison oak. You might see a gopher poking his head up from the ground; you'll certainly hear the sound of water not far away. In fall, there are wild grapes—look for the tangled vines.

From here, an overgrown bit of path leads toward a small waterfall you can't quite get to. You'll be stopped by a dense hedge of wild roses—and lots of poison oak. Back on the trail, you'll soon come to a crossroad and the cattail-fringed upper pond. There are houses on the hill up ahead, but you'll lose them as you start circling the pond, seeing only hilltop stables and greenhouses and, way off to the east, snow-capped mountains, a bit of a surprise on a hot winter's day.

At 1.5 miles, you'll reach the top of North Santa Fe Avenue. Turn left quickly and follow the trail back out of civilization and into the tules.

Notice the freshwater clam shells scattered near the creek crossing, the remains of many raccoon dinners. Ahead, the trail is lined with mustard and wild radish, and the country scents of fennel and horse manure perfume the air. Just before 2 miles, take the high road, bearing right. Where the road forks again, bear left, and as the trail rises, near the old fence, left again. You'll be heading back, somewhat steeply, downhill—watch your step.

At 2.5 miles, cross the willow-shaded creek to some nice sittable rocks, perfect for picnics. Here, in winter, you can watch the willows bud. If you stay long enough—a few weeks or so—you'll see the "pussy willows" turn to green or yellow catkins, followed by fluffy seeds. Even if you don't plan to picnic, this is a lovely rest stop.

Continuing on, turn right at the next fork, and cross the creek again; wild roses bloom here in spring. Farther on, watch the open areas for the speedy ground cuckoos called roadrunners. Seen standing still, they're much nobler-looking than their cartoon namesake, with their "Mohawk" crowns, long tails, and red-and-blue eye patches.

Stay on the main trail, bearing left at the forks. Soon you'll see the ranger residences and campground and, at 3 miles, rejoin the main service road. Go left, passing the head of the nature trail on your right.

As the soil gets saltier, notice the predominance of salt marsh plants, like pickleweed and gray-green Australian salt bush, a favorite perch of meadowlarks. Back in the 1880s, salt bush was introduced as cattle fodder in hope that San Diego's skinny cows could be fattened up enough to make richer milk. The cattle ignored the salt bush and kept producing natural low-fat milk, a century too soon for the anti-cholesterol craze.

Just ahead is the end—and the beginning—of the trail, where picnic tables, restrooms, and your car are all waiting for you.

BY THE WAY...

Rancho Guajome Adobe (TB11:B2)

About 1.5 miles south of the North Santa Fe park entrance is the "Cadillac of Adobes," built by Cave Couts and his Indian work force. The entrance, poorly marked, is easy to miss; look for a red-tiled kiosk and make a right turn at the bus stop and mailboxes just ahead. If you get to the forking roads, you've gone too far.

The adobe, in a sad state of disrepair but still evocative of the past, is open for free tours at 2:00 p.m. on Saturdays and Sundays. (For a nominal charge, group tours can be arranged on weekdays. Call 565-3600.) Ask to see the "Bat Room," off the old main entrance, where a large colony of small furry bats hangs, squeaking, from the ceiling.

Antique Gas and Steam Engine Museum (TB11:B2)

The entrance to the museum at 2040 North Santa Fe is easy to spot; there's a big tractor out front and an even bigger sign. Twice a year, in June and October, the popular Threshing Bee and Antique Engine Show takes place here, demonstrating farm equipment, crafts and techniques of bygone days. Founded in 1976, the museum includes 40 acres of farmland and over 1000 different items, and is dedicated to the preservation of the rural ways of early California. It is open daily from 10:00 a.m. to 4:00 p.m. For additional information, call 941-1791.

Dixon Lake Recreation Area

◆

LOCATION:

Escondido. Take I-15 north to El Norte Parkway, then go east to La Honda Drive. Turn north and follow La Honda to the park entrance (TB18:A4).

HOURS:

6:30 a.m. to sunset. $1.00 parking fee on weekends.

DESCRIPTION:

Owned and operated by the city of Escondido, Dixon Lake is an attractive reservoir surrounded by 527 acres of green grass, rolling hills, and shade trees. There are three picnic areas with tables and barbecues, playgrounds and horseshoe pits, and a campground. Fishing for trout, bass, and catfish is popular; the required state license and day permit are obtainable at the concession near the ranger station.

Rowboats and motorboats are available for rental, and Dixon Lake has good facilities for the handicapped; restrooms, picnic sites, and the pier near the ranger station all have handicapped access.

A nature trail leads through the primitive section of the grounds. If you like peace and quiet, it's best to avoid summer weekends.

For camping, boating, and group picnic reservations, call 741-3328. For other information, call 741-4680.

HISTORY:

Dixon Lake was named for James B. Dixon, son of a failed citrus grower who came to Escondido in the late 1800s and started a new and

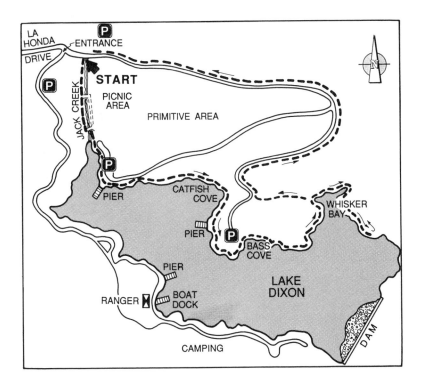

successful citrus nursery. Known locally as "Mr. Water," Jim Dixon was for many years Superintendent of the Escondido Water Company, and one of the first to envision a reservoir here, close to the small dam at Jack Creek that his father had built to provide more water for his trees.

The site was a good choice, high enough to allow water to flow by gravity, thus eliminating the need for an expensive pumping system. The dam, 100 feet high, was built in 1972; the reservoir was opened to the public in 1977. Over 90 percent of its water comes from the Colorado River.

◆ The Walk
DISTANCE: 3.5 miles round trip. TIME: 2 hours.

Park in the small lot a few hundred feet from the entrance, or, if this one's full, go through the primitive gate just beyond and park in the lot to your left.

Look for the rock-lined nature trail to the right of the gate; you should find trail guides in a wooden box nearby.

Fishing at Dixon Lake. Photo by Barbara Moore

Walk through a grove of acacia trees, covered with yellow flowers in early winter and stringbean-like seed pods in spring. Cross the service road and continue on, between picnic areas #1 and #2 and over a small wooden bridge. This is a nice, shady bit of trail, which you'll appreciate if you come on a hot summer day, when the temperature can climb to over 100 degrees.

Ahead is a big rock overhang, which we like to imagine was a shelter for Indians or perhaps the Dixon boys 100 years ago; look at the smoke-blackened walls. There's a bench where you can sit beside the canyon and listen to the waterfall below, just a trickle in summer, more serious after winter rains.

At about 0.3 mile, the trail forks. Go left downhill to the mouth of Jack Creek, named for the jackrabbits that were once plentiful here. Take the steps down, curve left, and cross the wooden bridge over the creek.

To the right, just after the crossing, is another bench where you can sit by the water and contemplate the sometime waterfall.

We go left, past mulefat, cattails, and, in fall, bright spots of red California fuchsia. On your right, look for mossy resurrection plant, brown and dead-looking in dry seasons until rainfall turns it a lively green.

Continue along, bearing right up the wooden erosion control steps. At the top, go right again, unless you've had enough, in which case the left-hand path will lead you back to picnic area #2.

We head on toward the dam, going down a stone stairway, and staying off the vehicle road. Bear left into the trees, and a lovely, shady part of the trail overlooking the green water. There are blackberries trailing down the hillside in fall, and fishermen trying their luck in the lake year-round.

The trail winds up and down through the willows, bypassing a fishing pier. Keep an eye out for the resident osprey that likes to perch on the telephone pole to the right of the dam.

In fall and winter, look for Bonaparte's gulls. They're the only local gull that dives for its dinner; all others are scavengers. Walk between the mauve plumes of fountain grass, and listen for the laughing sound of pied-billed grebes on the lake.

Just over a mile, before you round the turn to the next pier, there's a small grassy area at the water's edge that's perfect for picnics. Even if you're not thinking of food, you might want to sit beside the shoreside willow and the pampas grass and stare at the lake for awhile.

In spring, look for the purple flowers of showy penstemon and, on the hills, lots of blue ceanothus. You can, if you wish, take a detour to the Catfish Cove pier; we keep circling the lake.

At about 1.5 miles, there's a broad view of the dam and the mountains behind it, and you start through a drier section of trail, mostly broom and buckwheat. If you're out in the early morning or late afternoon, you might see mule deer on the hillsides; raccoons, coyotes, and the occasional fox or bobcat have been sighted here. Even if you don't get to see any of them, look for their tracks as you walk along.

Circle Whisker Bay, a popular trout-fishing spot fringed with pampas grass.

Pass the next left-forking road and walk on through overhanging sumac and willows, up and down the gentle hills, toward the ultimate portapotty—one with a commanding view of the lake.

Just over 2 miles is as far as you can go. There's another nice picnic spot here, on the flat rocks by the water's edge, just before the buoy line. We're told this is a good place to fish for catfish. Ahead is the 100-year spillway, designed to withstand even our legendary 100-year floods, and the dam.

When you're ready to leave, retrace your steps about 0.2 mile to the

Crossing Jack Creek. Photo by Barbara Moore

end of the "U" of Whisker Bay, and head up to the ridge for a speedy return trip. It won't be as pretty a walk, or as shady, but you will get a bird's-eye view of the lake.

Bear right onto the vehicle road at the top of the trail; the road to your left only leads to a parking lot. If you want a little more lake, you can head downhill farther on and pick up the nature trail again; otherwise, you'll be back at your car in about 20 minutes.

Lake Hodges

LOCATION:

Del Dios. Take I-15 north to Via Rancho Parkway; turn left. After several miles, turn left again to Lake Drive. The entrance gate is on Lake Drive between Beech and Ash lanes, next to the community park. Park in the lot near the concession, about a mile in from the front gate (TB27:B1).

HOURS:

Sunrise to sunset, Wednesday, Thursday, Saturday, and Sunday, March through November.

DESCRIPTION:

A popular fishing lake, Lake Hodges is a city reservoir operated by the San Diego Water Utilities Department. Fishermen must have a valid California license and a day permit, available at the concession. You can rent a boat at the pier or launch your own, for a small fee. Windsurfers are allowed on the lake in summer. For landlubbers, there are a few picnic tables and barbecues, and you can borrow horseshoes from the ranger. Portapotties are strategically located around the lake, and there are several interesting and little-used hiking trails. For walkers, a fine time to visit is after 3:30 p.m. on Tuesday or Friday, when the entrance gate is opened so fishermen can line up their vehicles at the second gate. You can park nearby, walk in, and have the whole place to yourself. In general, fishermen don't walk much, so there won't be much traffic on the trail. This is a good place to come when the coast is thick with fog; the sun is almost always shining here. For additional information, call City Lakes, 390-0222.

HISTORY:

Indians camped here in prehistoric times, finding plenty of the gray-green felsite rock they used to make their tools. There's an old ceremonial site nearby, where faded pictographs can still be seen.

The reservoir itself was the brainchild of Colonel Ed Fletcher, pioneer water, land, and road developer. In 1911, searching for a steady water source for his coastal developments, he made his way inland on foot from Rancho San Dieguito, following the riverbed until he found the ideal spot for a dam.

Financed by the "land improvement" branch of the Santa Fe Railroad, the dam was completed in 1918 and named for W. E. Hodges, vice president of the railroad. Bought by the city of San Diego in 1925, the lake was opened for fishing shortly after.

◆ Walk 1 Lake View Trail: North Shore Road to Felicita Cove
DISTANCE: 5 miles round trip. TIME: 2 hours.

A favorite of local joggers and bike riders, this wide road is never very crowded, and offers fine views of Lake Hodges and the surrounding hillsides. Start at the east end of the parking lot and head for the hills of Rancho Bernardo, following the fire road through meadows of buckwheat, sparsely dotted with trees. It's quite pretty here in spring, when

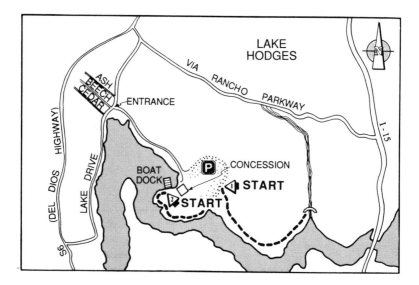

yellow bushy beardtongue, red monkey flower, and purple and white ceanothus are at their best. In summer, you'll see flashes of yellow tarweed, fennel, and prickly pear cactus flowers, and the small red blossoms of chalk-leaf dudleya.

There are usually a few snowy egrets or great blue herons down by the water, where the shore is lined with willows. In early morning or late afternoon, you may see a raccoon, coyote, or mule deer, or a family of quail skittering across the hillsides. This is snake country, too; keep an eye out for the yellow-banded black king snake, the slim, pink rosy boa, or the less approachable rattlesnake.

In the spring of 1988, there was a large brush fire out here that burned out of control for several days. The black tree skeletons and fire-scarred hillside may look depressing, but the green shoots sprouting up from underground burls show that things are still very much alive (see A Word About Chaparral, p. 36). Just a few months after the fire, the hills were covered with purple phacelia, magenta four o'clock, yellow monkey flowers, and white sage. And the wildflower displays for the next few years should be terrific.

At just over a mile you'll see a large group of pale buildings in the distance: a retirement home at the foot of Mule Hill, where General Kearny's starving troops sat down and ate their mules nearly a century and a half ago.

About 0.5 mile ahead, to the right, is a bunch of beehives. Don't tease the bees: they're erratic little buzzers, and can get edgy. Domestic honey bees were introduced to California from the Old World in 1850, when a few hives were sent around Cape Horn. Most of our natives are solitary bees that refuse to live in colonies; collecting honey from them is next to impossible.

At about 2 miles, take the rough path down toward the lake shore, where we like to stop for a moment to listen to the assortment of bird and cricket calls, and the distant hum of the freeway. Instead of heading straight up to the main road, take the small path north, through the stand of eucalyptus, pepper, willow, and oak trees. There you'll discover pretty little Felicita Creek, burbling cheerfully down from Felicita Park in Escondido.

There are several good spots for creekside picnics here—but be sure to check first for poison oak.

At the creek crossing up ahead, you can cross over and follow the lakeside road all the way to the freeway, or stay on this side and head left uphill and back to the parking lot.

◆ Walk 2 The Narrows Walk
DISTANCE: 2 miles round trip. TIME: 1 hour.

Walk past the dock, following the paved road to its end. Try a little birdwatching; you should see turkey vultures flying overhead, looking, from a distance, like drunken hawks. They're a lot more impressive on the ground, if you catch them hunched over a meal, and get a good look at their bald heads, long red faces, and pale bills. In the water, look for coots, grebes, and cormorants. Near the first boat launch, there are usually a number of ducks and geese, who may waddle noisily up to you, hoping for a free lunch.

About 0.5 mile from the parking lot, just after the second boat launch, the trail begins. Climb up the small hill and take the narrow path to your left. Where the path forks, there are pink and magenta sweetpeas blooming in spring. Follow the upper trail through redberry, toyon, lemonade berry, sagebrush, and the ever-popular buckwheat. In spring and summer, the white sage is particularly noticeable; its flowers look like tiny white orchids with tentacles.

On your right, by the water, are large clumps of tules, California's version of the bulrushes baby Moses was found in.

After you duck past the pepper trees and the tall broom, you'll come to a tule-fringed cove. There's a grassy area here, and a shady willow tree; this would be a nice place to picnic. If you're not in the mood for food, take time out to examine the tules. Notice the triangular shape of their stalks. There's an old saying: "Sedges have edges and rushes are round." Though called bulrushes, tules are obvious sedges.

Continuing uphill, keep out of the poison oak alongside the trail. As summer approaches, look for chalk-leaf dudleya. Its small flowers look very much like the lance-leaf dudleya found in lower elevations, but its stalk curves down from the top and its leaves are whiter. In fact, if you touch one of the leaves, a white chalky powder will come off on your fingers, and you'll see how the plant gets its name.

At about 0.5 mile in, you have to step gingerly through a cactus patch. If you're feeling adventurous, slide down the short, steep hill just ahead and follow the fishermen's trail through the tules. Being not terrifically sure of foot, we generally give it a miss, taking the left-forking trail heading uphill and back to the cove.

This higher trail gets a bit rougher and more overgrown, but it does give you a good view of the lake. If you're not up to a little mild bushwhacking, you can always go back the way you came; walk up a few yards for the view before turning around.

There are a number of small paths here, all leading back down to the same place. Whichever you choose, keep watching for poison oak. Past the tules, you'll have to beat your way through a short stretch of broom and poison oak; a walking stick is helpful here.

The ferny-looking plants that you see on both sides are ragweed. Most people are not allergic to the West Coast variety, which blooms in

Lake Hodges

104

late summer, not our sneeziest season. If you start choking up, you'll
know you're one of the exceptions.

This part of the trail sounds fraught with hazards, but actually it's
kind of fun. Take the last step down to the grassy cove and stay for a picnic, or walk on back to your car.

Felicita Park

LOCATION:

Escondido. Take I-15 to Via Rancho Parkway. Go west 1 mile to
Felicita Road, then north to the park entrance (TB27:E1).

HOURS:

9:30 a.m. to 5:00 p.m. $1.00 parking fee.

DESCRIPTION:

Fifty-three acres of rolling hills, shade trees, and flat grassy areas,
split by a pleasant year-round creek, this pretty county park offers family
and group picnicking, playgrounds, horseshoe pits, and covered dance
pavilions. The ranger will open the tiny museum, with its birds' nests, Indian artifacts, and historical photos, for interested groups. There are two
nature trails, the Ipai Trail and the North Creek Nature Trail; ask at the
ranger office for printed trail guides. For group reservations, call County
Parks, 565-3600.

HISTORY:

For hundreds of years, Felicita was the site of an Ipai village. It had
all the features the Indians prized: a reliable water source, a good supply
of acorns, and convenient granite rocks on which to grind them.

Felicita was the name of a chief's daughter who nursed a wounded
American soldier back to health after the Battle of San Pasqual. An annual pageant, something like the Ramona Pageant, used to be performed
in her honor.

◆ The Walk

DISTANCE: 1.5 miles round trip. TIME: 45 minutes.

Since the two nature trails are short, we like to combine them into
one satisfying double loop.

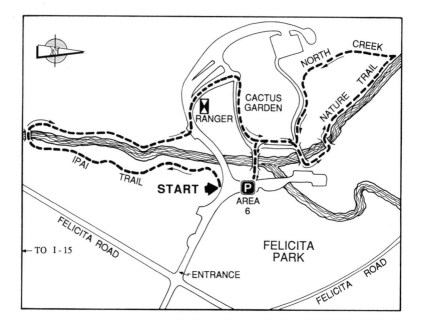

Park in the first lot at Area 6, and walk back to the stop sign, crossing the main road that leads to the upper parking area. Pick up the Ipai Trail to the left of the creek.

Besides live oaks, there are fan palms, sycamores, and lacy-leafed pepper trees along the trail. The palms were originally "planted" by birds and coyotes that ate the fruits whole and left the pits behind in their droppings, giving the seeds some instant fertilizer.

Look for gopher holes on the trail, and all over the park. They're covered with mounds of freshly dug dirt, which is how you can tell them from the uncovered holes of ground squirrels. Hawks and owls keep an eye on both kinds of holes, watching for a meal.

At about 0.25 mile, you'll see some of the granite boulders typical of the area. Continue around them to the path that leads down to the shallow creek. It's easy to cross without getting your feet wet; just look for a likely spot.

On the other side, heading back along the creek, stop near marker #4 to admire the little waterfalls. On a quiet morning, you might find a hawk or a raven taking a bath. Notice the bowl-shaped grinding holes in the gray rocks where, for centuries, Ipai women went through the tedious business of turning acorns into flour—drying, shelling, pounding, sifting, and pounding some more. The bitter tannic acid had to be leached out with water before the flour could be cooked into mush. The whole process could take days, but grinding was a social affair, a good time to catch up on the latest gossip.

Leaving the grinding holes, follow the rock-lined path uphill to #1, and the trail's actual beginning. (Yes, we've taken you backwards again.) From here, cross the parking lot to the "WALK—Park Office" sign. Take the steps up toward the ranger's office, then the graveled path past the newly planted cactus garden and down toward the first parking lot. Walk left along the creek to the second small bridge, close to the restrooms, at about 0.9 mile. After wet weather, you can find dozens of odd-looking mushrooms growing under the live oaks—look, but don't taste.

The graveled path leads to a third bridge and the start of the self-guiding North Creek Nature Trail. As you head uphill, past arroyo willows and other streamside vegetation, notice how fallen trees and stumps have sprouted new life from their dead trunks. In early spring, if you look carefully, you'll find a few tiny ferns, but it's easier to spot the wild

Indian grinding holes

cucumber vine, with its large green leaves and small white flowers, twining its curly tendrils over everything. By summer, the vines are dry and stringy, almost invisible.

A few hundred yards in from the trailhead is a wildlife observation area where a convenient bench faces several nesting boxes and bird feeders set in the trees. Ash-throated flycatchers, bluebirds, woodpeckers, and house wrens may be seen here in spring, and it's always a good spot for a quiet moment.

Down by the creek, look for water striders cruising along in search of food. The feet of these insects have water-repellant hairs that allow them to skim the surface so they are actually walking on water.

Leaving the creekside and heading uphill, you'll pass more grinding holes. With the help of the information plaques, stop and compare the Engelmann oak with its neighboring coast live oak. Both are live oaks—that is, they don't lose their leaves in winter—but the Engelmann's leaf is larger and more oval, while the coast live oak has small, notched, cupped leaves. Coast live oaks have slim acorns; Engelmann acorns are round and fat.

From here, we move into an open section of buckwheat, chamise, and sage. In season, there's a beautiful assortment of wildflowers here; the wine-red peonies are particularly striking in early spring.

At 1.4 miles, pick up the paved path heading down to Area 6, and, perhaps, a nice post-walk picnic. Take a look at the big sycamore beside the toddlers' playground; its soft wood is full of woodpecker storage holes. Starlings, house wrens, and woodpeckers all use this tree for their hollowed-out nests. Barn owls like to perch in the branches; on the ground below, you can often find owl pellets containing tiny gopher skulls and bones.

Lake Poway Recreation Area

LOCATION:

Poway. From I-15, take Rancho Bernardo Road east. After crossing Pomerado, Rancho Bernardo becomes Espola. Continue on Espola to Lake Poway Road. Turn left and drive to the entrance booth (TB33:D3).

HOURS:

Park open daily, sunrise to sunset. Lake, Wednesday through Sunday, 6:00 a.m. to sunset. Parking is free to Poway residents. Others pay $3.00 weekdays and $4.00 weekends.

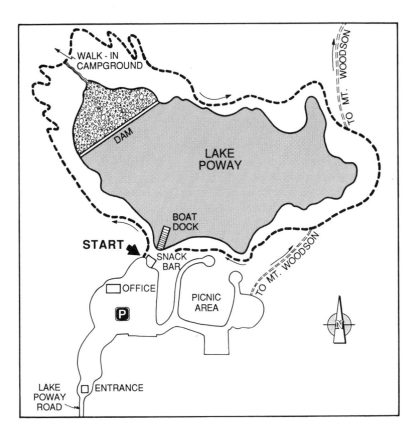

DESCRIPTION:

This fine lake (man-made, of course) and its surrounding wilderness area are owned and operated by the city of Poway, which has plans for a major system of hiking and equestrian trails, designed to connect residential neighborhoods with parks and open spaces. Daily fishing permits and state licenses may be purchased at the concession, which sells film and duck food too. You can rent a boat here or launch your own.

There's a walk-in campground near the northwest corner of the lake, and a dock and equestrian staging area to the south. There are also playgrounds, volleyball courts, horseshoe pits, a softball field, and nice grassy areas for picnicking. It can get hot out here in summer, and cold in winter. If you plan on walking, dress accordingly. In summer, carry drinking water. For further information, call 748-2224.

HISTORY:

Poway, incorporated as a city in 1980, took its name from an old Indian word meaning, it is thought, "meeting place of the valleys." Since there were year-round streams, cattle from the San Diego Mission were grazed here. The dam was completed in 1971, creating the 60-acre lake.

The 405 acres of undeveloped land around Lake Poway are named in honor of Clyde E. Rexrode, first mayor of Poway, who devoted himself to preserving its open spaces.

◆ The Walk
DISTANCE: 3.5 miles round trip. TIME: 2 to 2.5 hours.

Drive past the water treatment plant, pay your fee, park in the lot, and pick up the trail to the left of the snack bar (open Wednesday through Sunday). If walking isn't your only interest, you can stroll out on the floating dock and fish-watch, or rent a boat, or feed the ducks. You might just want to sit down on a bench along the first short stretch of trail and survey the lake before you start hiking. We did.

The broad trail soon narrows. The rock triangle you see in the notch between the mountains to the north is the newly built (1988) Ramona Dam. The narrow stone strip in the foreground is Poway Dam, which is fenced off. The trail we are following, the Warren Canyon Trail, goes around the base of Poway Dam, which is as close as you can get.

A sign will inform you that you're entering the Rexrode Wilderness

Family outing

Area. Don't be put off by the steep beginning—just take it easy and enjoy the view.

Bear right at #1 on the old nature trail, heading into the ever-popular sage scrub. Look for turkey vultures flying over the water. From the distance, they look like large dark hawks, but they don't glide as smoothly, and their wings are more V-shaped.

Keep bearing right, and follow the signs toward the campground. Watch your step on the downhill—a walking stick is helpful here if you're not very sure of foot. Stick to the main trail, ignoring the offshoots; in late spring, look for fleabane, a small yellow-centered lavender daisy, thought to be a natural flea repellant. It must work, because the last time we were here, we didn't see a single flea, though we were bitten by almost every other insect known to man as we made our way down to the foot of the dam. In the small buggy creek where willows, cattails, and poison oak grow, look for Hooker's evening primrose in spring and summer. These showy yellow flowers are named for the 19th-century botanist who was director of the Royal Botanical Gardens at Kew, near London.

At #4, there's a watering trough, which sometimes doubles as a birdbath. Nearby is a hitching post, if you want to rest your pony.

The trail continues downhill. At about a mile, there's a fork in the road; we like to go left down the steep road to the shady campground for a picnic break or a drink of water. There are restrooms, tables, and barbecues but rarely any people here, and you can admire the live oaks and sycamores, and the lone pine by the side of the babbling but mostly invisible brook.

Back on the road again, go up to the fork and start heading left up and around the lake. It really feels like a wilderness here, as you tramp past rocky boulders under a serene blue sky, heading away from the dam. At about 1.5 miles, you start heading toward it again, climbing all the way; the views into the distant hazy mountains are a kind of compensation.

About 2 miles from the trailhead, you come to the top of the dam and start seeing the lake again. A bit farther on, you emerge from the Warren Canyon Trail and start left around the lake, back on the wide trail.

At Pine Point, another nice spot to consider for a picnic, you'll see your first portapotties, and a fish scale, if you've got anything to weigh. On the hillsides above the second pair of portapotties—well, not *all* the trail's features are scenic—you should see blue ceanothus and red heart-leaf penstemon, if you're here in the spring. As you start uphill again, you'll get a good view of the small coves of Pine Point.

Bear left at the top of the hill and take the lower and wider of the two trails going past the information kiosk. The milepost says 1 mile to the end of the trail; you can make it.

Hooker's evening primrose. Photo by Barbara Moore

Again, there's a bit of a climb, but after the half-mile marker, it's downhill all the way, bearing right and heading toward the grassy area by the boat docks.

If you haven't picnicked yet, consider stopping here. If you're not tired, the trailhead to Mt. Woodson is near the equestrian staging area. It's a more strenuous undertaking—but don't let us stop you.

Dos Picos Park

LOCATION:

Ramona. Take Highway 67 north to Mussey Grade Road, then go south 1 mile to Dos Picos Park Road, which ends at the park entrance (TB33N:E4).

HOURS:

9:30 a.m. to sunset. $1.00 parking fee.

DESCRIPTION:

A backcountry county park with shady live oak trees and a pleasant campground, Dos Picos is a popular place for group picnics. A small man-made lake attracts wild and domestic waterbirds, and many other species frequent the 78 acres of woodlands and chaparral. There are playgrounds, horseshoe pits, and a jogging parcourse, in addition to ample facilities for picnics and barbecues. There's also a tiny but interesting collection of butterflies, skulls, and dried flora at the ranger station near the campground entrance. For additional information and reservations, call County Parks, 565-3600.

HISTORY:

Named for the two mountain peaks most easily seen if you're driving down from Julian, Dos Picos was inhabited by Ipai hundreds of years ago. In 1961, the county acquired the property for a park; originally, it was to be given an Ipai name, but somehow, as in history, the Spanish prevailed.

◆ The Walk
DISTANCE: 2 miles round trip. TIME: 1 hour.

Unless you're camping, you'll have to park at the picnic area and pick up the nature trail behind the campground. Start at the little wooden bridge at the southeast corner of the lot and head for the maniac squawking of geese; when you hear them, you'll know why some people use them

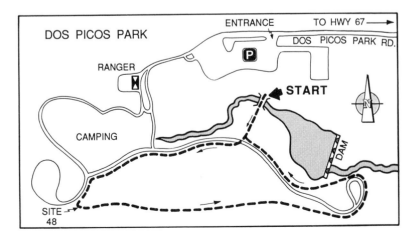

Yerba santa

instead of guard dogs. Take a little detour to the pond if you're in a feeding mood or want to inspect the water for tadpoles; otherwise, take the dirt road heading west, following the parcourse, passing a log jungle gym and slides, and leading toward the campground. Watch out for red ants here and elsewhere on the trail; they can crawl up bare legs and bite!

With all the oak trees around, you should see some black-and-white acorn woodpeckers. There's a large and varied bird population in the park, so keep your eyes open.

It's about 0.5 mile to the start of the nature trail, between the caravan area and site #48. The trail climbs a bit at first, but soon levels out; in this direction, the walk is mostly downhill.

Watch out for poison oak, and look for round red galls on the scrub oaks. Though they look like apples, they're really a kind of tumor, formed by the plant in response to a small, stingless wasp. The wasp secretes a fluid that triggers formation of the gall, which serves as food and protection for its eggs until the larvae are ready to go out into the world. Each of the 2000 American species of gallmaking insects has its own specific plant host.

As you walk along, you'll have a number of opportunities to look out at the mountains and wonder which of the peaks might have been the two for which the park was named. Closer at hand, notice the lichens and mosses growing on the north side of the rocks, where it's generally cooler and damper. Lichens are really a combination of two different plants living together in that state of mutual benefit called symbiosis. One of them, a type of blue-green algae, converts sunlight into food through photosynthesis. The other, a fungus, shelters the alga and keeps it from drying out.

You'll see plenty of the ubiquitous buckwheat, its flower clusters pink and white in spring, rust-colored in fall. At #9, there's an example of mountain mahogany, an unlikely looking member of the rose family. It has dark, wedge-shaped leaves, and is most noticeable in late summer and fall, when it's covered with slim, curling white feathers that extend from its seeds.

Number 10 is yerba santa, the "bandaid bush." Indians used its soft gray leaves to cover wounds and staunch the flow of blood. At #11, in spring, you'll see ceanothus—wild lilac—in bloom. The white variety is fairly unremarkable, but the blue does resemble miniature lilacs.

Just beyond, about a mile in on the trail, is a junction. You can go downhill to your left and shortcut back to the jungle gym, the pond, and the parking lot, or continue on to the wider dirt vehicle road, and head right for a detour to the park's eastern boundary. If no youth groups are camping here, there's a peaceful live oak grove that could serve as a secluded picnic setting. On the other side of the fence is a corral of the Ellison Ranch, which raises fine quarterhorses.

Looking westward, the stone wall you see is the back side of the reservoir. You can start at its northern end and walk through the spillway, whose well-made walls and stone steps seem a rather ambitious project for such a small body of water. In a few minutes, you'll be rounding the pond again, just a goose-honk away from the parking lot.

Note: On Highway 67, near town, you can buy fresh eggs, game meats, produce, and plants. Ramona, named for Helen Hunt Jackson's romantic novel, has an interesting relationship with animals. It used to be the turkey capital of the West and currently has a llama as honorary mayor.

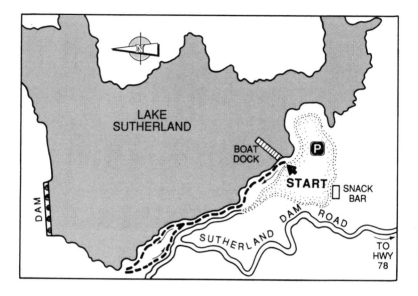

Lake Sutherland

◆

LOCATION:

Ramona. Take I-8 east to Highway 67. Go north to Ramona and take Highway 78 east to Sutherland Dam Road, which leads to the lake entrance. Drive down toward the boat dock and park in the upper lot just below the concession (TB405:B1).

HOURS:

Sunrise to sunset, Friday through Sunday, March through mid-October (subject to change).

DESCRIPTION:

A beautiful and relatively unvisited city reservoir, Sutherland is ringed by Indian reservations, an agricultural preserve, and the Cleveland National Forest. It offers good fishing, a small, tree-shaded picnic area, snack bar/concession, boat launch, and a dock where rental boats are available. At present, there are portapotties scattered around the lake; regular restrooms are planned.

This is a good place to look for wildlife: eagles, osprey, deer, and even bobcats are not uncommon. A primitive campground is in the works for the near future. For information, and to confirm hours, call City Lakes, 390-0222.

HISTORY:

Centuries ago, the area around Santa Ysabel Creek, Sutherland's main water source, was inhabited by Indians; there are grinding holes in the rock outcroppings not far from the dock.

The dam was begun in 1929, but financial and political problems postponed its completion until 1953, when the lake was opened to the public for fishing.

The dead trees on both sides of the dock were healthy willows until 1978, when 46 inches of rain overfilled the dam, drowning the willows. Receding water left the sad-looking skeletons you see today on what was once a green and pleasant stretch of shoreline.

In recent years, the water level has declined drastically, dropping as much as an inch a day. By the end of 1988, the reservoir contained only 10 percent of its normal volume.

◆ The Walk

DISTANCE: 2 miles round trip. TIME: 1 hour.

From the parking lot, take the upper dirt road north alongside the live oaks until it forks after 100 feet or so, heading toward the dam.

In spring, the hillsides here are covered with mustard and blue ceanothus. In summer, there's telegraph weed in bloom. The tall stalks topped with small yellow flowers are a sure sign of a disturbed area.

Year-round, look for the resident golden eagle flying overhead. It likes to perch in the dead trees on either side of the boat dock, where you may also see an occasional osprey, which looks like a large hawk, or the distinctive profile of a kingfisher, with its big crested head and small body.

In the water, you can usually see a great blue heron or two; ducks and geese come by in late fall, and so do duck hunters. While you're watching for birds, stay out of the deposits of illegally grazing cows, supposed to be restricted to the east side of the lake.

At about 0.8 mile, you can follow the trail down to a little-green island, revealed only in times of low water; there are some Indian grinding holes here too. If the water's too high, or you're not in the mood, continue on about another 0.1 mile till you come to a crossroads.

Here, you have three choices:

1. Take the right-forking path toward the dam, which looks like a wall of 17 slanting silos, and is said to be one of the most earthquake-

proof dams around. Built on a 45-degree angle, it's even more fascinating seen from behind. If you're a dam fan, special group tours can sometimes be arranged with the dam keeper.

Bear left at the bottom of the path, continuing on through rows of mulefat. If you smell something pungent, it's epazote, an herb that does wonders for Mexican beans.

The trail fades away, but without much trouble, you can make your way down to the water's edge, across usually dry, cracked salt flats that feel as if you're walking on styrofoam. There are some comfortable rocks where you can sit and enjoy the view—if the water's low enough.

2. Stay on the road another 0.25 mile for a closer look at the dam. You can go as far as the buoy line; after that, access is restricted.

3. Go uphill and into the trees, and start circling back. Here, you'll be walking through live oaks, Engelmann oaks, and red-barked manzanita; on a hot day, of which there are many out here, you'll be grateful for the shade.

There are fine views down to the lake as you continue uphill for a short way, along the eroded trail that soon joins the paved vehicle road. Then you start downhill, picking up a wide dirt road to your left after about 0.2 mile.

Again, you'll meet the main road, briefly, and again take the dirt road left, and back down to the parking lot. Keep an eye out for cars here; this is the main exit road.

You can stop for a drink at the concession stand, or picnic on the hill just behind it—it's time for a break!

Lake Sutherland

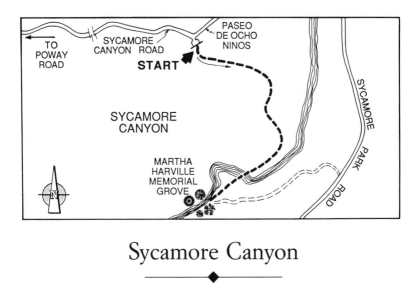

Sycamore Canyon

◆

LOCATION:

Poway. From I-15, go east on Poway Road to Garden Road. Turn right, go past Garden Park and turn right on Sycamore Canyon Road. Continue on 2.3 miles to a locked gate. The trailhead is just to the left of the gate by an information kiosk (TB37N:B5).

HOURS:

Sunrise to sunset.

DESCRIPTION:

These 857 acres of county-owned land have only recently been opened to the public as a regional park. It's a fine place for long and short walks, with chaparral-covered hills and canyons, impressive views, shady groves, and all sorts of wildflowers. The trail, newly made, is the first part of a planned system of hiking/equestrian trails from Poway to Santee. Someday—the Parks Department budget will determine how soon— there will be trails running all through the valley, connecting into Santee Lakes and Mission Trails Regional Park. The main staging area is planned for the Santee side about 1.3 miles south of Highway 67, but, for now, the best way in is from the Poway side, where there is some parking. It can get hot out here, especially in summer, so dress accordingly and carry water. To date, there are no facilities.

HISTORY:

Centuries ago, this area, with its then year-round water source and steady supply of live oak acorns, was an Indian campsite. In the late 1800s, a group of German farmers settled here and founded the tiny town of Stowe. Fifteen families grew oats, wheat, and other crops, and built their own school and post office, of which not a trace remains. The town died in 1906, when the families went their separate ways. Later, the Gooden Ranch, near the Poway entrance, raised alfalfa to feed the horses at the Del Mar Racetrack. The property was recently bought by developers who are turning it into 50 or 60 ranch-style homes.

◆ The Walk

DISTANCE: 3 miles round trip. TIME: 1.5 to 2 hours.

There's room for a few cars to park just outside the Sycamore Canyon Road gate. Step over the log barrier to the left of the gate, check out the information kiosk, with its good-sized map of the area, and head on up the trail.

In spring, the hillsides are covered with the yellow of sunflowers, rock rose, golden yarrow, and the tall shrubs called bushy beardtongue. There's lots of blue ceanothus too; the flowers of this inland variety are much bluer than those near the coast. The buckwheat here grows like trees; this is full-scale chaparral, not the softer, lower-growing coastal sage scrub.

The path climbs steadily but gently, offering good views of the old Gooden Ranch, soon to become as much a part of the invisible past as the short-lived town of Stowe. The pale green ground cover whose white flowers look like hundreds of tiny eyes is rattlesnake weed, also known as squaw purge or golandrina, which means "swallow." It's said to cure rattlesnake bites.

At 0.1 mile, near the top of the first rise, step up on the large flat rock, and see if you can see, in the notch of the distant mountains, a silver sliver of Santee Lakes. Someday, this trail will run all the way out there. For now, content yourself with finding a few landmarks. Cowles Mountain is the tallest peak to the left, with a little antenna on top. Next highest, to the right, is Fortuna Mountain. Both are part of Mission Trails Regional Park, to which this trail will also connect, someday.

After the rise comes a downhill stretch. Then the path undulates up and down, changing your point of view on the surrounding scenery.

At about a mile, there's a pleasant oak-shaded spot with a dry creekbed that starts flowing after winter rains. This would be a good place for a picnic or, even better, try the larger grove about 0.2 mile farther on. This second, the Martha Harville Memorial Grove, was named for a young park ranger who helped develop the park and asked that her ashes be scattered here. You'll find benches, and to the left of the trail,

Nature study. Photo courtesy San Diego Natural History Museum

some old grinding holes. Look for the bowl-shaped indentations in the rocks where Indian women spent long hours pounding acorns into meal.

Owls roost in these trees. Look on the ground for their pellets, the fur balls they spit out, with the tiny skulls and bones of their rodent dinners still inside.

In spring, there are wild roses blooming. Lean over to catch their sweet scent, but stay on the trail and out of the poison oak.

The creekbed here is where the Stowe Post Office is said to have been, not that anyone has managed to find any sign of it. The end of the woodsy area, at about 1.5 miles, is a good turnaround point. If you feel like going on, you can continue all the way up the proposed staging area at the top of the hill—about another 5 miles. The return trip is mostly uphill, so take your time.

Incidentally, rangers tell us that there are several rare plants growing in these parts: San Diego thornmint, mesa clubmoss, copperleaf, and chocolate lily. We didn't see any of them; maybe you'll do better.

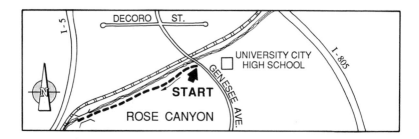

Rose Canyon Hiking Park

◆

LOCATION:

University City. Take I-5 north to La Jolla Village Drive. Go east to Genesee Avenue, then south to Decoro Street, where you can park. Walk south about 0.2 mile along busy Genesee to the park entrance, across from University City High School. (TB44:E3).

HOURS:

Always open.

DESCRIPTION:

With 275 acres of open space surrounding the old roadbed of the Santa Fe Railroad, Rose Canyon is a pleasant oasis in one of the fastest-growing areas of the city. There are no facilities.

HISTORY:

In 1769, Gaspar de Portola, military commander of the Sacred Expedition that brought Father Serra to San Diego, rested his men here on their way up north. A hundred years later, the area was named for Louis Rose, a Texan who came to San Diego in 1850, tanned hides in the canyon, acted as Old Town postmaster for 10 years, and developed a community called Roseville in what is now the business district of Point Loma.

◆ The Walk

DISTANCE: 3 miles round trip. TIME: 1 to 1.5 hours.

Follow the broad maintenance trail along Rose Creek, which flows into Mission Bay. Across the creek is the "new" roadbed of the Santa Fe Railroad.

The first wooded section of trail is the nicest. In winter, when the

A WORD ABOUT STREAMSIDES

San Diego definitely has its ups and downs. Our high table-top mesas are split by rugged canyons and broad valleys that were carved out by eons of runoff water, creating a complex drainage system of rivers and creeks that flow into the sea.

In the bottoms of these canyons and valleys we find what is called the streamside or riparian (riverbank) plant community. Even where the streams are only seasonal, there is still enough water to support large, thirsty trees like sycamores, coast live oaks, and cottonwoods. All plants drink and eliminate water, much as we do, and sycamores are particularly heavy drinkers. A single tree needs 300 gallons a day to survive—that's six bathtubsfull!

San Diego's streamsides are some of its pleasantest locations. Besides the trees, there are tall leafy shrubs like arroyo (creek) willows and mulefat, and water-loving plants like wild roses, California fuchsia, and, less welcome, but undeniably pretty in autumn, poison oak. Foxes, bobcats, deer, raccoons, and many smaller animals and reptiles find these areas good places to live, with plenty of water, food, and shelter. In spring, resident hawks, owls, and woodpeckers share the trees with colorful migrants like orioles, flycatchers, and tanagers.

Indians, too, found streamsides attractive. They liked to set up their camps near water, gather acorns from the live oaks, and use convenient granite boulders for acorn grinding. Centuries of patient pounding hollowed out bowl-like depressions in the granite, sure signs of Indian presence.

In their natural state, streamside communities change slowly, but increasing development of our mesa tops has created new problems—erosion from overwatering; introduced exotic plants like pampas grass, acacia, and thistle, that spread quickly and threaten the survival of natives; and neighborhood cats and dogs that prey on wildlife.

Today, major highways arc over the streamside canyons, or cut right through them. Since they are the lowest places in the county, storm sewers have been installed beneath them, the tell-tale manholes showing at intervals along the jeep roads built to maintain them. An ignominious fate, perhaps, for our streamsides, but these are the paths we walkers usually follow.

sycamores are bare, you can easily see the large stick nests of hawks and owls. Owls start nesting in February; if you notice a catlike face staring at you from a treetop nest, it's a great horned owl. They usually raise three

Autumn in the sycamores. Photo by Bill Evarts courtesy San Diego Natural History Museum

or four chicks that resemble fuzzy tennis balls when they first hatch. One nest may be used interchangeably year after year by owls, hawks, and ravens.

By June, you'll see many immature hawks, bigger than their parents, exercising their wings by flapping and jumping up and down near their nest. Once we saw a pair of redtails working out so vigorously on the edge of their nest, they actually knocked it out of the tree.

Starting at 0.3 mile on the right is a large patch of nightshade, a tomato relative with gray leaves and pale blue flowers in spring, and tiny round yellow fruits in fall and winter. Also in spring, there's lots of fennel, yellow mustard, and pink thistle, as well as exotic escapees from the hilltop yards.

As you continue into the open area, houses and the railroad tracks come more into view. Despite these intrusions, most of the canyon is pretty quiet, except for the occasional rumble of passing trains.

With all the "Golden Triangle" development just to the north, what's left of the local wildlife has been forced into the canyon. In spring, particularly, watch for rattlesnakes, which seem to like it here.

About 1.5 miles in, you'll reach the remains of an old wooden railroad bridge, at the foot of the powerlines. From here on, the sounds of I-5 traffic overwhelm the sounds of bird calls—as good a time as any to start heading back.

San Clemente Canyon

LOCATION:

University City. From Highway 52, between I-5 and I-805, take Regents Road/Clairemont Mesa Boulevard south to the park entrance, circling right under the bridge to the east parking lot (TB44:D5). To shorten the walk somewhat, use the alternate entrance at Highway 52 and Genesee Avenue (TB44:F5).

HOURS:

Always open.

DESCRIPTION:

Bounded by freeways, San Clemente has over 400 wooded acres to explore. There are picnic tables, barbecues, and restrooms near the Clairemont Mesa Boulevard entrance, restrooms near the Genesee Avenue entrance, and benches scattered along the trail. If there's been any significant rain, try another canyon; too much water can make crisscrossing San Clemente Creek more of a wade than a walk. In fact, you might not even be able to drive into the parking lot.

HISTORY:

Legend has it that San Clemente was originally named Cañada Clemente or "Clemente's Glen," after the Indian caretaker of the vineyards, orchards, and gardens planted here by the padres. Somehow, over the years, the canyon, if not Clemente himself, was canonized.

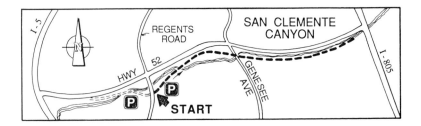

Today, San Clemente's official name—Marian Bear Memorial Park—honors the woman who persuaded Caltrans (the California Department of Transportation) and the city to build Highway 52 on the canyon's higher, dryer south side, saving most of its coast live oaks and sycamores from destruction.

◆ The Walk

DISTANCE: 6 miles round trip. TIME: 2 to 2.5 hours.

Park in the east parking lot and follow the broad dirt vehicle road heading east. In early spring, neighborhood kids slide down the grassy slopes on strips of cardboard. Later in the season, park crews mow the grass to reduce fire hazard.

On your left, in the creekbed, are tall old sycamores, shorter arroyo willows, and mulefat, once a prime food source for mules and cattle. Some of the finest sycamores in town are in this canyon—green in spring, gold in autumn, white skeletons in winter. Keep an eye out for poison oak, which twines in vast quantities around the sycamores. One of us managed to get a rash from just brushing up against some dried winter twigs, so watch where you swing your arms.

As you walk along, notice the cockleburrs. They stick to anything they touch—dogs, clothes, each other—and are said to have inspired the invention of Velcro. Cockleburrs use their stick-to-itiveness to spread their seeds. Taking no chances, they have two kinds of seeds—one for this year and one for next—in case there's not enough rain to start the first batch growing.

There's lots of horehound here too. A member of the mint family, it has leaves like a geranium and flowers like a sage, stems of white clusters that turn to brown seed pods in fall.

Even though the sounds of traffic never quite disappear, you can still manage to hear the tapping of striped black-and-white Nuttall's wood-peckers busily probing the porous bark of the sycamores for insects. These woodpeckers have long barbed tongues, good for getting into small crevices to spear their hors d'oeuvres.

Turn right at the large two-trunked sycamore at about 0.4 mile, just before the first creek crossing, and take the narrow path uphill and into the live oaks. After a bit, there's a short, steep descent—maybe 6 feet or so—that can be a little tricky to negotiate when muddy, but if we can make it, so can you.

This is a prettier route, farther from the traffic, but you can stay on the main trail if you prefer.

Follow the creek eastward through the oak woodlands. In early spring, you'll notice the fuchsia-flowered gooseberry, whose small red flowers look like cultivated fuchsias. They're followed by hairy berries that birds and foxes love to eat. Indians added the berries to meat to make pemmican, a staple food for long trips and hard times. By June, this thorny bush is leafless; more obvious then are the wild roses, tiny red geraniums, and lavender checker-bloom.

The trail leads slightly uphill to your right, rejoining the main trail within sight of the Genesee Avenue overpass. You'll be crisscrossing the

San Clemente Creek

creek and walking along several long stretches of cobbles.

These cobbles are Mexican immigrants, formed by a volcanic episode that occurred about 45 million years ago, near what is now Guaymas, in Sonora, Mexico. They were carried here by an ancient river with the help of the same continental plate movement that created the Sea of Cortez and the San Andreas Fault. Local Indians found these smooth rounded rocks just the right size to use as pestles for grinding seeds and acorns.

At about a mile, cross under the overpasses, taking the path closest to the creek. Look in the small ponds for mosquito fish, planted in spring to keep mosquito larvae under control. You may also see the eggs of fresh-water snails on the undersides of leaves floating in the water, and masses of frog eggs on the surface. In late spring, these hatch into tadpoles; the tiny ones become tree frogs, the larger ones, bull frogs.

Up ahead, you'll rejoin the main service road. Going left uphill leads to restrooms and the Genesee Avenue parking lot. We go right along the cobbles and then head east.

A few years ago, when San Clemente's storm sewers were upgraded, the canyon floor was dug up and hydroseeded with a wildflower mix to prevent erosion. Unfortunately, nobody thought to choose seeds of *local* wildflowers, so most bloomed for a season and died. One of the survivors was common yarrow, with its soft ferny leaves and 3-foot-high flower stalks. Another survivor was fuller's teasel, a somewhat taller thistlelike plant. Fuller is an old word for cloth-maker, and the bristly seed pods were used in Europe years ago to card wool. You can see some fuller's teasel near sewer standpipe "Y," at about 2 miles. Here, you can rest on a bench amid the ragweed, looking up toward the live oaks, and listening for the sound of crickets.

You can follow the trail for another mile, until it loops around a small stand of live oaks near I-805.

Tecolote Canyon Natural Park

LOCATION:

Clairemont/Linda Vista.

For Walk 1: Clairemont. From I-805, take Clairemont Mesa Boulevard west to Genesee Avenue. Turn left and go one block to Bannock; turn right and park near North Clairemont Park and Recreation Center (TB44:F6).

For Walk 2: Clairemont. From I-805, take Balboa Avenue west to Genesee Avenue. Go south to Marlesta Drive, opposite Mesa College.

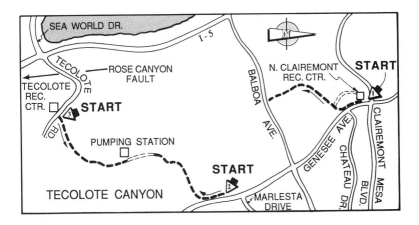

Park north of the traffic light—there's no parking up ahead—and walk 0.25 mile to the park entrance (TB53:B3).

For Walk 3: Linda Vista. From I-5, take the Sea World Drive exit. Go east on Tecolote Road about 0.2 mile to Tecolote Canyon Park and Recreation Center (TB59:F1).

HOURS:

Always open.

DESCRIPTION:

At over 900 acres, Tecolote is one of our larger urban canyons. It is unusual because it runs north to south, rather than east to west, as most streamside canyons do. *Tecolote* is a Mexican word for "owl," and there are definitely owls living here, along with hawks and many kinds of songbirds. Keep your eyes open for poison oak, especially in less traveled areas.

There are restrooms, picnic tables and barbecues, ballfields, basketball courts, and a playground at the Tecolote Park and Recreation Center. There are similar facilities at North Clairemont Park.

HISTORY:

Tecolote has been on the map for 200 years and shows evidence of 2500 years of Indian residence. Until 1953, cattle were grazed near the mouth of the canyon, which was used as a gravel pit during the building of I-5. In 1957, when the city decided to dump landfill in the canyon and turn the gravel pit into a city operations yard, the first community

Willow buds

protests began. They went on for 18 years, until Tecolote was finally set aside as an open space park, a victory that led to the preservation of our other urban canyons. Local residents, originally asked to contribute to the purchase of Tecolote, later had their money returned by the city. Many refused the refund, instead using the money to reintroduce native plants into the canyon.

◆ Walk 1 Chateau Drive Trail
DISTANCE: 3.5 miles round trip. TIME: 1.5 hours.

Whether you approach from the south end of the North Clairemont Park and Recreation Center, descending a steep hill strewn with bits of broken glass, or stroll southward 0.4 mile past the roar of Genesee Avenue traffic, or try to dash across in front of that traffic from Chateau Drive to the park entrance—access to this trail leaves something to be desired.

However you manage to get there, the peaceful feeling of Tecolote's shady creekside glades takes over almost immediately. This is our favorite walk in the canyon.

Live oaks predominate. Notice their holly-notched cupped leaves and, in fall and winter, the slim pointed acorns. As you stroll along, you'll see a number of attempts at erosion and flood control: bark chips on the trail, gabions on the creekbank, rocks laid in feeder creeks to form all-weather crossings for maintenance vehicles.

In late winter, you may be lucky enough to see a pair of kites engaged in their pre-nuptial flights. Their courtship ritual involves the male passing a dead mouse to his chosen female in midair. Usually, she accepts, they eat together, and then mate. If she turns him down, he'll eat the mouse himself, and try again later.

Grey and white, with black shoulder patches, kites get their name from their habit of "kiting" on the wind, floating down to their prey instead of diving like other hawks.

You can walk all the way south to Balboa Avenue. We turn around a few hundred feet sooner, before the sounds of traffic get a chance to register.

◆ Walk 2 Marlesta Trail
DISTANCE: 2.2 miles round trip. TIME: 1 hour.

Here again, getting to the trailhead is the only bad part of this trip; you have to walk south alongside the Genesee Avenue traffic. Once you're on the trail, though, you can relax among the live oaks, sycamores, and willows, crossing back and forth over Tecolote Creek.

Coming down from Genesee, take the first creek crossing and then bear right. In fall, look for the red tubular flowers of California fuchsia. Although there's lots of poison oak, you can still find some nice picnic spots among the trees beside the water. The last time we were here, there were more crayfish in the creek than we'd seen in any one location—and that was in the dry season!

At just over a mile, the trail narrows. Ahead is our turnaround, the driving range of the golf course.

◆ Walk 3 Tecolote Recreation Center Trail

DISTANCE: 4 miles round trip. TIME: 1.5 to 2 hours.

The most suburban of Tecolote's walks also offers the most conveniences, including easy access and ample parking.

To begin, walk through the gate at the east end of the Rec Center's parking lot, following the wide dirt road between the ballfields and channelized Tecolote Creek. Streamside vegetation here has been replaced with cement to control flooding. Surrounded by housing developments and the University of San Diego, this is surely the best-known of Tecolote's trails.

In spring, the area is bright with yellow chrysanthemums, locally known as "Caltrans daisy" because the seeds were inadvertently spread by the highway department's road-grading equipment. There are lots of introduced plants in the canyon, including a few century plants with tree-high stalks.

After awhile, the concrete channel gives way to more natural streamside vegetation, the canyon widens and the houses become less obtrusive. There's a small live oak grove to the left named for canyon activist Marian Bear and, at about 1.5 miles, a recently planted section funded by local residents.

In spring, you'll see golden poppies, California's state flower. Here the creek's flow is interrupted by gabions, stone-filled wire sediment traps—another attempt to control flooding and erosion.

We usually turn around at the gas pumping station just before 2 miles, but you can go all the way to Clairemont Drive if you want, passing the Tecolote Golf Course up ahead.

BY THE WAY...

Back at the Rec Center, you may want to take a quick look at the Rose Canyon Fault, which runs from Mexico into the sea at La Jolla Shores, paralleling the infamous San Andreas Fault part of the way.

Walk westward along the fenced baseball field, then uphill to the upper ballfield. Leaving the pavement where the path forks, follow the fence 20 yards or so, noticing how abruptly the dirt bank on your right changes from cobbles to sandstone. The fault is where the change occurs, separating the 500,000-year-old cobble/dirt conglomerate from the 50-million-year-old Scripps Formation sandstone. Unprepossessing though it may seem, this is one of the few places you can actually see an earthquake fault up close. Most are now covered over by buildings, bushes, and blacktop.

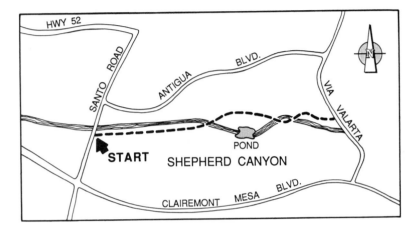

Shepherd Canyon

◆

LOCATION:

Tierrasanta. Take I-15 north to Clairemont Mesa Boulevard. Go east to Santo Road, turn left, and park about 0.2 mile in, near the trail sign (TB46:B6).

HOURS:

Always open.

DESCRIPTION:

This walking and jogging trail is a surprisingly pretty and peaceful place overlooked by new development and the playing fields of Tierrasanta Municipal Park. Technically speaking, Shepherd Canyon lies somewhat to the north, but we've never heard this canyon called anything else. There are no facilities.

Chaparral broom in bloom

HISTORY:

The area including Shepherd Canyon was once part of Camp Elliott, a 13,000-acre marine training camp used during World War II for artillery and tank training. Unexploded shells may still be found here. Anything suspicious looking should *not* be touched; it could still be dangerous. It's highly unlikely you'll find any ordnance along the trail, but if you do, mark the location, and call 911 as soon as possible.

◆ The Walk

DISTANCE: 2.5 miles round trip. TIME: 1 hour.

Arroyo willows and several varieties of eucalyptus line the trail, along with the usual coastal sage scrub. The willows stay green until winter, when they turn golden, providing a sweep of post-fall color. Then they start shedding their leaves, form buds, and go into their spring cycle.

There are several spring wildflowers here that we've rarely found in our other locations. Starting at about 0.8 mile, look for purple sage, an introduced plant with soft, textured gray leaves and pinkish flowers. In winter, you'll notice the tall stalks of dried seed-pod clusters. To the right, in early spring, star lily starts blooming, knee-high stalks of white star-shaped flowers appearing among the tall, grasslike leaves.

There's enough chaparral broom along the trail to try a little study of plant sex. In autumn, look closely at the broom in bloom. Contrary to what you might expect, the slim, white, hairy flowers are female; the male flowers are rather flat and fuzzy.

At about 0.7 mile, you'll come to a concrete spillway, on the other side of which is a catchment pond. If you go right here, you can scramble uphill to the park for a quick jog around the parcourse. We go left and head up toward the houses.

Bear right at the fork for a willow-framed view of the pond, where blackbirds, warblers, and sparrows often stop by for a drink. The gray-leafed shrub that looks almost like white sage is brittlebush, another introduced plant more commonly seen in the desert. Related to bush sunflower, it has bright yellow spring flowers.

Going downhill, you get away from the houses and into a pleasantly wooded section with a real country feeling. Bear right uphill and around, following the creek from above. The trail undulates up and down (mostly up) to a T intersection. This is our turnaround, though you can continue another 0.1 mile or so to Via Valarta, an alternate point of entry.

Along the Mission Trail: San Diego Mission and the Old Mission Dam

◆

LOCATION:

Mission Gorge.

Mission San Diego de Alcala. Take I-8 east to Mission Gorge, then go left under the freeway to Twain Avenue, and left again. Twain Avenue becomes San Diego Mission Road; the mission and its parking lot will be on your right (TB54:B5).

Mission Dam. Take Mission Gorge northeast to Junipero Serra Trail; turn left and continue about 1.5 miles till you see the "Mission Trails Regional Park/Old Mission Dam" sign on your left (TB47:A5).

HOURS:

San Diego Mission, 9:00 a.m. to 5:00 p.m. $1.00 entrance fee. Mission Dam, sunrise to sunset. Note: Junipero Serra Trail is closed to vehicle traffic from sunset to sunrise.

DESCRIPTION:

A two-stop trip, combining Spanish-era history and a look at some of the wide-open spaces of Mission Trails Regional Park, said to be the larg-

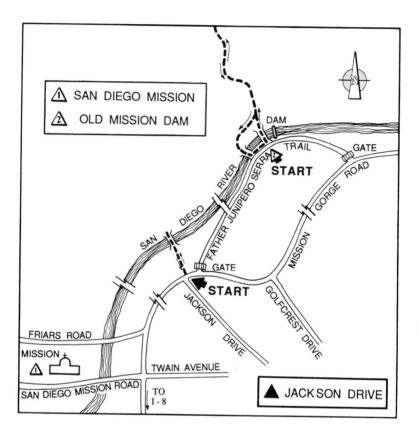

est urban park in the U.S. The Mission San Diego de Alcala—"The Mother of the Missions"—has been restored to a kind of splendor it never really had. Beautifully landscaped, its grounds are a delightful place to spend an hour. There are restrooms, drinking fountains, and a small gift and bookshop. Taped tours are available, and guided group tours may be arranged on request; call 281-8449. The dam area offers wilder walks, through more natural surroundings. Aside from a few picnic tables, there are no facilities.

HISTORY:

The first of California's 21 missions was actually a brushwood shack on Presidio Hill, built under the direction of Father Junipero Serra, shortly after the arrival of the Sacred Expedition of 1769.

Moved to this site because of its nearness to the river and its distance from the Spanish soldiers, who couldn't keep their hands off female converts, the rebuilt mission was a second brushwood shack. It was burned and pillaged in 1775 by hundreds of local Indians who didn't appreciate the attempts at their conversion. Father Luis Jayme, killed in the uprising, is buried under the sanctuary. The rebellious Indians sank into the dim mists of history; the Spaniards went on with their conquest.

The mission was rebuilt of less flammable adobe, but its checkered career continued. Damaged by earthquakes, secularized by Mexicans, and later occupied by American soldiers, it was wholly in ruins by the turn of the century. It wasn't till the height of the Depression, when the Spanish period began to take on a rosy glow, that the mission was restored and rededicated. Today, it's a working parish church, as well as a tourist attraction.

The old Mission Dam, built between 1813 and 1816, is a registered national historical monument. It was the first major irrigation project on the West Coast, the start of California agriculture, and the beginning of the end of the unhindered flow of our rivers.

◆ **Walk 1 Mission History Stroll**
DISTANCE: 0.25 mile. TIME: 30 minutes.

Admission includes an information brochure and map, and you're welcome to wander through the grounds, admire the gardens, and visit the sanctuary, chapel, and museum. There are informative plaques all over, many of the plants are labeled, and docents in the gift shop are happy to answer any questions you have about mission history.

Inside the church, to the left of the altar, just under the papal umbrella and opposite the small statue of Father Serra, is a dark painting of San Diego de Alcala, said to have been brought here by Serra himself. San Diego, or St. Didacus (rhymes with Leviticus), was a 15th-century Spanish Franciscan. A hundred years after his death, when the son and heir of King Philip II lay dying, he was put to bed with the "incorrupt" body of the old priest and miraculously cured. Philip petitioned Rome on Diego's behalf, and sainthood was granted in 1588, a bad year for the Spanish Armada.

Arriving here on Diego's feast day 14 years later, Vizcaino renamed the area in honor of his saintly compatriot. Today, despite continuing controversy, Father Serra, too, is well on his way to beatification.

In the small museum are a few relics of San Diego's past, an inexplicable display of New Mexican Indian pottery, and pictures of the mission before its restoration. Outside, in the main quadrangle, are excavations of the old rooms of the monastery, the project of a U.S.D. archaeology class in the late 1960s. You can sit under the pepper trees by the fountain and listen to the murmur of the water and the freeway traffic, contemplating the vagaries of history, and the romanticized version of it all around you. Try to envision the surrounding hillsides as they really were a few hundred years ago, all chaparral and silence.

This is a good place to study the birds and the bees. Look for native goldfinches and hummingbirds near the fountain, and imported Mediterranean honeybees buzzing around their hives in the South American pepper trees. Don't forget to walk up the arcade before you leave and look in on the pomegranate, citrus, peach, and loquat trees in the garden of the Virgin of Guadalupe.

Leaving the padres' headquarters, we head upstream to see their greatest achievement, the Old Mission Dam. It's amazingly peaceful for something so close to busy Mission Gorge.

Right by the parking lot, overlooking the tamed San Diego River, are a number of our native trees; take a few minutes to look at their leaf shapes, and you'll never again confuse a cottonwood with a sycamore or a willow. Cottonwood leaves are heart-shaped, and seem to "twinkle" in

Mission San Diego de Alcala. Photo by Barbara Moore

the wind; sycamores have maple-shaped leaves; and black willow leaves are slim, like knife blades. Don't expect to have much luck with your leaf study in winter, since cottonwoods and the white-barked sycamores are deciduous, and usually bare by December. All these trees are good for birdwatching, especially in the morning and late afternoon; look for woodpeckers, warblers, and goldfinches.

◆ Walk 2 Mission Dam Trail

DISTANCE: 1.5 miles round trip. TIME: 1 hour.

Walk in on the short stone path, lined with recent plantings of wild roses, pink and fragrant in spring, bright with red-orange rosehips (their Vitamin C-rich seed pods) in fall; baby sycamores and live oaks; and golden California poppies, our state flower.

Just ahead is a forest of Hooker's evening primrose, whose large yellow flowers bloom in summer; look for goldfinches eating their seeds in the fall.

Walk on past the unshaded picnic tables—personally, we'd rather lunch by the water—and down to the old dam where, today, water flows gently and people fish quietly for bass and catfish. Walk carefully along the water-worn rocks to the left of the dam, or avoid the smooth, slippery things entirely by taking the main path west past the picnic tables and turning right at the Mission Dam plaque.

Either way, you'll have to follow one of the vague paths around the riverbank to a somewhat unsteady log across a 6-foot stretch of shallow water. A walking stick gives you a third leg for balance; just take your time—you don't get points for style. (If it's too muddy, or the water's too high, or this just isn't your idea of a good time, go back to the main trail, and do this walk backwards, using the sewer pipe bridge.)

Once you're on the other side, the hard part is over. You can climb up the rocks to your right for a nice view from higher ground, or simply take the left-forking path into the shade and walk north on level ground, along the Oak Canyon Trail that follows the creekbed.

In fall, look for red California fuchsia among the buckwheat, broom, and white sage. Live oaks, sycamores, and mulefat line the creekbed, and there are raccoon and deer tracks on the trail, along with the usual coyote "calling card"—grayish, fur-filled droppings.

You can picnic under a spreading creekside oak tree at about 0.5 mile. In winter, when the creek is full, there are hundreds of tadpoles here.

Bear left at the fork at about 0.7 mile, and head into the trees for another great picnic spot. Unlike many of these shady places, there doesn't seem to be too much poison oak around. Another 0.1 mile on, there are rocks that can turn into a waterfall after winter rains.

We turn around at the flat rock outcropping a few hundred yards

Old Mission Dam. Photo by Barbara Moore

above the creekbed here, where splotches of chartreuse lichen and green moss make the rocks look like a painter's dropcloth, and it's so quiet, you can hear an acorn drop. Look for Indian grinding holes—we found a few.

Follow the trail back the way you came, but just before you get to the dam, instead of bearing left and going across the log again, bear right, following the north bank of the river, pushing through the mulefat, stepping over a few fallen trees—trust us, this isn't as bad as it sounds—until, at about 1.3 miles, you reach the sewer-pipe crossing that soon should be covered by a wooden bridge. Cross over, and you're headed right back to the parking lot.

If you haven't picnicked and you're ready for refreshment, there's a country-style restaurant a few miles east at Mission Gorge and Mast Street. The best thing about it is the free iced well water!

Down by the Riverside: Jackson Drive

◆

See map on page 136.

LOCATION:

Mission Gorge. Take I-8 east to Mission Gorge Road; stay on Mission Gorge until the traffic light at Jackson Drive. Turn left and park in one of two small clearings on the north side of the street (TB54:F2).

HOURS:

Always open.

DESCRIPTION:

A bit of quiet chaparral beside a busy thoroughfare, Jackson Drive is a good place to come for a short walk in open country. Down by the narrow river, there are several nice spots for waterside picnics. There are no facilities.

HISTORY:

This city-owned section of Mission Trails Regional Park lies deep in the gorge carved out by the once-mighty San Diego River, first dammed by the padres in the early 1800s. The aqueduct they built ran through here, carrying water from the dam to the mission down in the valley.

More recently, Jackson Drive has become a "mitigation area," planted with mulefat and willows by the city in return for permission to invade the upstream habitat of the endangered least Bell's vireo during restoration work on Mission Dam.

Such tit-for-tat ecological balancing is required by the U.S. Fish and Wildlife Service. The new habitat is seven times larger than the old one, but the birds haven't gone for it yet.

◆ The Walk

DISTANCE: 1 mile round trip. TIME: 30 minutes.

Park in one of the inconspicuous parking areas, walk in through the gate, and follow the wide vehicle road into the gorge. This is the maintenance road for the second aqueduct built in 1960 to bring more Colorado River water into rapidly growing San Diego. The two vertical pipes you see on top of the hill in front of you are ventilating towers for the aqueduct.

After about 0.25 mile, you leave the sound of traffic and start to hear water trickling over rocks. Up ahead, you can cross the narrow, usually ankle-deep river on a series of stepping stones, not quite large enough to keep your feet completely out of the water. On the north bank, not far from the mitigation planting, you can picnic by a tiny "waterfall," surrounded by cattails, willows, and cottonwoods.

If you don't feel like getting your feet wet, look for three rusty vertical pipes to the left of the crossing and follow the little overgrown path just left of them across a cement-covered pipe to the river's south bank. You can sit on the rocks here and be just as happy.

City-planted poppies and phacelia bloom in spring, and year-round, you can watch ambitious mountain bikers pedaling up the steep hill to the northwest and intrepid rock-climbers making their way up the steeper rocks east of the gorge. We like to admire them all from afar.

To the east, the trail leads to Junipero Serra Trail; westward, you head toward a working quarry, grinding gravel for concrete buildings and freeways. You can wander off if you like; we usually prefer just staying by the water, eternally hoping for a glimpse of a small, slow-moving, olive-drab bird—the least Bell's vireo, which neither of us has ever seen.

Lake San Vicente

LOCATION:

Lakeside. Take I-8 east to Highway 67 and go north. Turn right on San Vicente Avenue and left on Moreno Avenue. Follow Moreno to the entrance of the lake. (TB42:F2)

HOURS:

Sunrise to sunset, Thursday, Saturday, and Sunday, October to mid-June. Same hours, Friday, Saturday, and Sunday, mid-June through September. $3.50/person entrance fee, summer only.

DESCRIPTION:

A man-made mountain lake whose pleasant surroundings are still untouched by development, San Vicente has only one drawback: It costs $3.50 per person to get in from mid-June to October, when the lake is reserved for waterskiing. It's a stiff price to pay for hiking, but it's usually too hot to go then anyway.

The rest of the year, there's no admission charge, and for a daily fee,

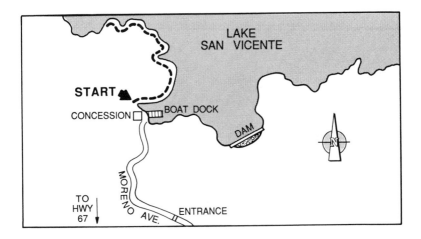

California-licensed fishermen can test their skill at hooking trout, bass, and catfish. Rental boats are available during fishing season. For reservations, call City Lakes, 390-0222.

Near the marina, you'll find a concession, open from 8:00 a.m. to 3:00 p.m., a small covered pavilion with a few picnic tables, barbecues, and restrooms. On the hillside southeast of the parking lot is another picnic area, and above it, a lookout tower, from which a ranger can keep an eye on the lake.

HISTORY:

San Vicente Dam towers 200 feet above the streambed of San Vicente Creek. Built by the city of San Diego in 1941–43, it stores water from Lake Sutherland, the Colorado River, and Northern California, as well as local runoff. The lake was stocked and opened to the public for fishing in 1949.

For several years, San Vicente has been supervised by Susan Parker, San Diego's only woman reservoir keeper. She came to work as a lake aide in 1982—a summer job before college—and she never left. She's part of a two-dam family; her husband is the reservoir keeper at Lake Sutherland.

◆ The Walk

DISTANCE: 2.4 miles round trip. TIME: 1.5 hours.

Drive up the road that winds through laurel sumac and buckwheat, and then drops down to the parking area and marina, about a mile from the entrance.

Fence lizard (top left) and alligator lizard. Drawings by David Stump

The trail starts to the left of the parking lot. Take the upper trail, a wide vehicle road opened to cars a few years ago when windsurfers were allowed on the lake. These days, this road to the abandoned wind-surfer launch is usually closed to traffic; it's a good place for a quiet, view-filled walk.

Where the road divides, at the top of the first hill, follow the red "Wrong Way" sign; you're not a vehicle, so you don't have to obey.

These dry, chaparral-covered hillsides are very susceptible to brush fires, as you can tell from the charred remains of shrubs and trees along the way. Before you get to feeling too bad about it, remember that chaparral fires encourage healthy new growth. As you walk on, the vegetation gets taller and thicker, with sumac, chamise, and scrub oak predominating.

There's a short paved stretch at about 0.9 mile. When the paved section ends, you cross over the rocks of a man-made waterfall, flowing just like the real thing, whenever water is pumped into the reservoir.

You'll see tall tree tobacco growing close by and, in summer, down by the water, splashes of magenta canchalagua. You may also see a great blue heron, or catch a glimpse of a pied-billed grebe building a nest in the cattails. Watch the hillsides for rabbits, snakes, and lizards—and the occasional coyote.

The road leads down to a picnic table (and portapotty) just at the water's edge. It's a wonderful place to sit and admire the lake and its myriad blue, red, and black-and-white dragonflies, sometimes called "devil's darning needles" because old folk tales say they can sew up the mouths of children who tell lies. This is one of the few places you can be all by yourself by the water, even on a holiday weekend. We found it easy to dream here, and hard to pick ourselves up and get back on the road.

Rounding the first bend on the return trip, you get a good look at the dam and start hearing the sounds of the world again. At about 1.9 miles, you can take the short, rocky drainage path down to the water and follow the fishermen's trail back. On a warm day, it's cooler down here, and you get a different perspective on the lake.

Lake Jennings

LOCATION:

Lakeside. Take I-8 east to Lake Jennings Park Road; turn left, then right onto Harritt Road. Where Harritt Road divides, go right to the south entrance. Drive in about 2.2 miles along the lake's main road and park where the pavement ends at Eagle Point (TB49:C3).

HOURS:

South gate, sunrise to sunset, Friday through Sunday. Night hours in summer. Campground, open weekdays, 9:30 a.m. to sunset, 9:30 a.m. to 9:30 p.m. on weekends.

DESCRIPTION:

Lake Jennings is an attractive mountain-ringed reservoir with a 100-acre campground at its northwest corner, and a boat pier, launch ramp, and concession to the south. Popular with fishermen, the lake is operated by the Helix Water District; a day permit and state license are required if you want to try your luck with trout, bass, and catfish. Rowboats and electric motorboats can be rented at the pier, or you can launch your own for a small fee. At present, there are no picnic facilities, but some are planned for the future. The Parks Department runs the campground, which is open to campers only. For reservations, call County Parks, 565-3600.

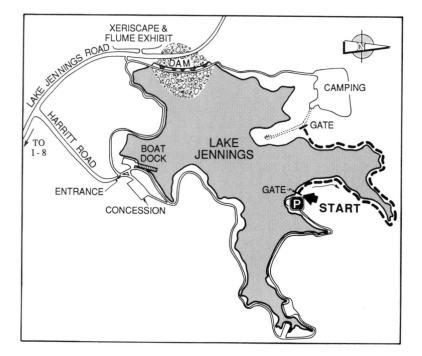

HISTORY:

Once part of the 49,000-acre El Cajon Rancho, Lake Jennings, like most of the county's lakes, is a man-made reservoir. The dam was built in 1962 by the Helix Irrigation District, and named for its first general manager, Chet Harritt. The lake was named for Bill Jennings, legal counsel for the H.I.D. and vice president of the California Water Commission.

◆ The Walk

DISTANCE: 3 miles round trip. TIME: 1.5 hours.

The lake's entire 5.5-mile circuit is open to runners and walkers; we settle for the unpaved portion, 1.5 miles gate-to-gate, following the wide dirt road toward the campground. Campers can start from the campground, and do the walk from the opposite direction. Either way, it's a pleasant stroll past laurel sumac, sagebrush, and large clumps of prickly pear cactus.

In spring, the flat spiny pads are decorated with waxy yellow flowers; the dark red oval fruits follow. Both de-spined pads and fruits were eaten by Indians and are still commonly sold in Mexican markets. In summer, look for cottony patches of cochineal scale, tiny insects whose bodies, crushed and dried, produce a natural red dye. Cultivated in Mexico for centuries, cochineal must be tediously handpicked, with 70,000 insects needed for every pound of dye. Before the development of modern coal tar dyes, cochineal colored pork sausages, soft drinks, cosmetics, and maraschino cherries. With coal tar dyes now linked to cancer, cochineal has been approved by the FDA and could be making a major comeback.

As you walk along, watch for quail, roadrunners, and maybe the pale horned lizard, popularly called a "horny toad," sunning itself by the side of the trail. In winter, you'll see yellow-rumped warblers flashing through the laurel sumac, whose seeds they love to eat. Sumac's dried flower clusters look rather like miniature trees, and they're sometimes used as such in architects' models and model railroad landscapes.

We saw our best and closest osprey sitting on a shoreline willow about 6 feet away from us, coolly surveying the lake. Also called fish

Lake Jennings

hawks, ospreys may be found around any body of water in the county, salt or fresh. Listen for their sweet chirping call, very unhawklike.

We turn around at the gate, where the paved vehicle road begins. You can take one of the small fishermen's paths down to the lake, if you wish, before heading back.

BY THE WAY...

Xeriscape Garden and Flume Exhibit

While you're at Lake Jennings, you may want to make a brief stop at the office of the Helix Water District, located on Lake Jennings Park Road, between the campground and the fishing entrance.

Outside is a small xeriscape garden, from the Greek *xeros,* which means "dry," as in Xerox, the dry copier. Xeriscapes are aesthetic arrangements of plants suited to dry climates, needing little maintenance and less water. This one includes Cuyamaca cypress, palo verde, sagebrush, rosemary, sage, and several types of ceanothus.

Across from the garden is a display of part of the old redwood flume, a 35-mile aqueduct built in 1889 to bring water down from the Cuyamacas to the thirsty citizens of San Diego.

At the flume's grand opening, everyone pronounced the mountain water a great improvement over the river water they'd been drinking. It later turned out that, for the first few weeks at least, they were drinking the same old stuff after all; engineers had forgotten to install air valves and had had to "borrow" river water until the problem was taken care of.

Indian flume-walkers were paid to wade barefoot along the length of the flume, plucking debris out of the water. They were allowed to keep any drowned animals they felt like eating. For awhile, flat boats were tied together and floated down the flume—a cross between a pleasure cruise and an amusement park ride.

A seven-year drought around the turn of the century dried up Lake Cuyamaca, but somehow the flume stayed in operation until 1936, when it was put out of business by the new, nearer El Capitan Dam and Reservoir.

Louis A. Stelzer Park

◆

LOCATION:

Lakeside. Take I-8 to Highway 67; exit at Maple View Street. Go east to Ashwood, which becomes Wildcat Canyon Road. The park entrance is 2 miles ahead (TB49:B1).

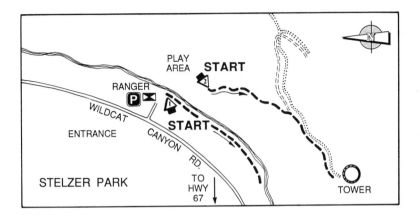

HOURS:

9:30 a.m. to 5:00 p.m. $1.00 parking fee.

DESCRIPTION:

This 314-acre regional park has special attractions for children and the disabled, but is a delightful place for any nature-lover to visit. Family and group picnic areas, youth group campsites, hiking trails, restrooms, and play areas are all designed to accommodate wheelchairs. The wheelchair-accessible exercise course is particularly imaginative, and enjoyed by able-bodied children too. For further information, call County Parks, 565-3600.

HISTORY:

Once a Kumeyaay campsite, the land was a family retreat for real estate magnate Louis A. Stelzer in the 1940s. It was left to the county on his death in 1971, along with additional funds for its development as a park with facilities for the handicapped. The park was officially opened to the public in 1983.

◆ Walk 1 Riparian Hiking Trail

DISTANCE: 1.3 miles round trip. TIME: 30 to 40 minutes.

To the right of the entrance is the Riparian Hiking Trail, which follows the seasonal Wildcat Canyon Creek about 0.7 mile to a hidden picnic site. Along the trail, masses of poison oak hang gracefully from the sycamores; rangers say the stuff here is really vicious and its leaves are, in

Camping at Stelzer Park

fact, as big as your hand.

The trail has gentler features: coast live oaks, wild grapes, and blackberries. Spring is especially pretty, with ferns, mustard, and wild radish in their glory, and wrentits, goldfinches, and rufous-sided towhees singing in the trees. Spring is also the time to look for patches of scarlet pimpernel, whose tiny star-shaped flowers are usually scarlet in England but mostly pale coral-colored here. A famous romantic novel written just after the turn of the century concerned a daring Englishman who outwitted the masterminds of the French Revolution and used the flower as his signature and pseudonym. Perhaps he chose the pimpernel because it was an old symbol of assignation. Known to close dependably in late afternoon and in cloudy weather, it has also been called "the shepherd's clock" and "the poor man's weatherglass."

The trail ends at a tree-shaded table, where you might want to spread out a picnic lunch.

◆ Walk 2 Stelzer Ridge Trail

DISTANCE: 2.2 miles round trip. TIME: 1 hour.

This trail is, in most ways, the opposite of Walk 1. While the Riparian Trail is flat and shady, this one is uphill and exposed—not the best choice on a blazing summer day. Still, it's not too taxing a walk, rather pretty, and certainly worth an hour of your time.

The first 0.5 mile is wheelchair accessible, as someday the whole trail will be.

To reach the trailhead, cross Wildcat Canyon Creek, turn right at the park's information kiosk, and walk past the play area, stopping if you want to check out the wheelchair fitness stations. The trail starts past the restrooms, just opposite a huge live oak tree whose low-hanging branches are great for sitting or climbing, depending on your age and agility.

The trail is a wide dirt path through live oaks into chaparral. In spring, the hillsides are dotted with lavender bush mallow; in summer, the white flowers of buckwheat take over, turning to rusty brown in fall.

At about 0.2 mile, opposite a dead live oak, is chaparral currant. In fall, look for its pink flower clusters; in winter, you'll see the purple berries, which are dry and bitter. Indians used the roots to relieve toothache.

Climbing gradually, you soon start getting good views of the surrounding mountains. The trail passes through a meadow of wild oats, green in spring, pale gold in summer. After the first rains, you can spot the bright green shoots of the next crop.

Spring wildflowers here put on a good show, with purple lupine and snapdragons, golden yarrow, and lavender mariposa lilies covering the hillsides.

At about 0.5 mile, you can take the narrow left-forking shortcut uphill; one way or another, the path is less wheelchair-friendly from here on.

If you're shortcutting, cross over the main trail once and continue uphill till the second crossing; you eliminate a few switchbacks this way before heading southward toward the powerlines.

At the ridge, there's an SDG&E service road. You could head left here and take the steep 0.5-mile climb to Stelzer Summit, but the view is no more rewarding than the one from Kumeyaay Promontory, and a whole lot harder to reach.

We head right, straight toward the power towers and sweeping vistas of Lakeside, Santee, and as far west as air quality will permit. You can get quite a feeling of power up here, looking at the toy landscape below—but then there's all the SDG&E power, towering over *you*.

If you feel like tackling the summit after this—good luck.

Silverwood Wildlife Sanctuary

◆

LOCATION:

Lakeside. Take I-8 east to Highway 67 in El Cajon, then head north to Lakeside. Turn right on Mapleview and left on Ashwood, which becomes Wildcat Canyon Road. From the last turn, it's about 5 miles to Silverwood; look for the yellow mailbox and stone gateway on the right side of the road (TB42P:D2).

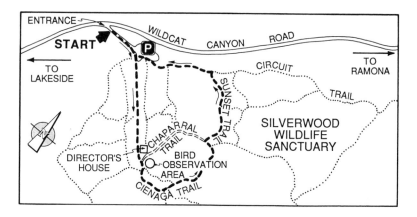

HOURS:

Sundays only, 9:00 a.m. to 4:00 p.m. Closed in August.

DESCRIPTION:

These 550 acres of chaparral are owned by the San Diego Audubon Society, which keeps them as close to their natural state as possible. There are several miles of hiking trails, at least 230 species of flowering plants, and 157 bird species. You can picnic near the shady bird observation area by the director's house or close to the parking lot. Volunteers lead guided nature walks every Sunday at 10:00 a.m. and 1:30 p.m. Organized groups can schedule special tours by calling 443-2998.

HISTORY:

Established in 1965, the sanctuary was a gift to the Audubon Society. During the Depression, Harry Woodward, a savings and loan executive, acquired the property by paying its back taxes. He built the small house now occupied by the director as a weekend retreat, and from 1934 on, kept careful notes on the plants and animals living in the area, including, in the 1940s, his sightings of California condors, probably the last ones seen in San Diego County. Woodward called the place Silverwood because of the silvery look of the sunlight on the leaves of the live oak trees.

◆ The Walk

DISTANCE: 1.5 miles round trip. TIME: 1 hour.

This trail combo is a good introduction to the varied joys of Silverwood. To start, a short 0.3-mile stroll leads to the director's house and the bird observation area, located by a seasonal creek.

Here you can sit on an odd assortment of donated furniture and watch the winged residents bathe and eat under the tall live oaks. If you enjoy birdwatching, come in the morning, when the feeders are filled. Later in the day, especially when it's warm, birds tend to stay hidden.

At the director's house, you can pick up a map of the park and its trails, copies of the Audubon newsletter, and an assortment of other information.

From the observation area, walk east past the green tank and follow the sign to the Cienaga Trail. You'll be leaving the shade and heading through chamise and mountain mahogany, easiest to recognize in late summer and fall, when it's covered with white, curly "feathers," the plumed tails of its seeds.

In spring, you'll be surrounded by scarlet delphinium, blue larkspur, and magenta canchalagua as you proceed into the cienaga, or marshy meadow, which can become marshy indeed after rain.

Silverwood is home to 30 mammal species, including foxes and coyotes, whose droppings you can see along the trail. In fall, the droppings are studded with reddish-brown manzanita berries—irresistible, but, apparently, not completely digestible.

A piece of the rock: Southern California batholith. Photo by Barbara Moore

After you cross the meadow the Cienaga Trail turns into the Chaparral Trail. Ahead on your right, almost hidden on the ground, is marker #27, where you'll find holly-leaf cherry. A member of the rose family, it has small whitish flowers in spring, and dark cherrylike fall fruit—a favorite food of many birds and animals. Indians ate them too, though they're really more pit than cherry.

Stay on the main trail, bearing left; #16 is sugar bush, or mountain sumac, a relative of laurel sumac and lemonade berry, whose tiny reddish berries are also food for birds.

At about 0.6 mile in on the Cienaga-Chaparral Trail is a junction; from here, looking north, you can see a Christmas tree farm across the valley. Bearing left will take you back to the bird observation area; we bear right onto the Sunset Trail, for a bit of local geology.

At viewpoint "A," just on the left, the cleft granite rock dates back to a time 100 million years ago when dinosaurs roamed the earth. Like the other rocks you've been seeing, it's part of the Southern California Batholith. The word batholith is a combination of the Greek words for depth—bathos—and stone—lithos. Our batholith was once a huge mass of molten rock lying deep beneath the ocean floor, extending from Los Angeles County all the way down into Baja California. As the sea level receded and the land rose, the massive rock was exposed to air; eons later, it remains a visible part of our topography.

At the foot of this venerable boulder, look for delicate bird's foot fern, whose leaf clusters look like tiny bird's feet. You should also find selaginella, a member of the spike moss family that dominated the coal forests millions of years ago, long before the appearance of flowering plants. Popularly called resurrection plant, selaginella looks dead most of the year but turns bright green and springs back to life as soon as it rains.

At "B," look northward to the big squarish rock on whose face is the setting sun for which this trail was named. This sunset is not a carved petroglyph or a fossil, but just one of the interesting patterns produced by ages of weathering.

Walk past the sunset—could it be a sunrise?—and follow the trail right, past more boulders and bird's foot ferns. Mosses and lichens on the trailside rocks can make this section quite pretty in winter and spring. Lichens are some of the oldest plants on earth; here's some doggerel to remember them by: "Annie Algae and Freddie Fungi took a lichen to each other and lived happily ever after in sinbiosis." As a sideline to their mutually beneficial relationship, the algae and fungi in each lichen species produce organic acids, which ultimately break down rocks into soil.

Bear left around a flat granite outcropping to "E," a possible Indian grinding hole, through it does seem far from the creek and rather solitary for the sociable activity of acorn-pounding. It could be a natural depression, made by rainwater and decomposing leaves.

After a view of Wildcat Canyon Road, the Christmas tree farm, and the distant mountains, make your way carefully downhill, staying on the Sunset Trail. Just head toward the sounds of traffic; at the fork, pick up the Circuit Trail to the left, which will take you back to your car.

William Heise Park

LOCATION:

Julian. Take I-8 east to Highway 67. Go northeast through Ramona, connecting up with Highway 78. At Santa Ysabel, Highway 78 joins Highway 79; continue on to Pine Hills Road. Turn right and follow the brown "Heise Park" signs to Frisius Road. Turn left on Frisius and go another 2 miles to the park entrance (TB405:E3).

HOURS:

9:30 to sunset. $1.00 day-use fee.

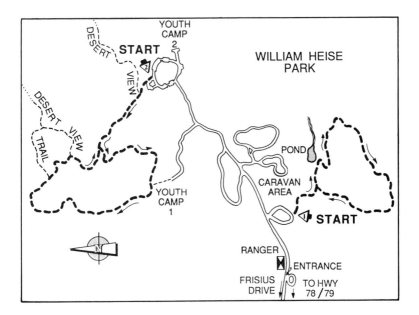

155

DESCRIPTION:

William Heise Park includes almost 1000 acres of pine and oak woodlands on the northern edge of the Laguna Mountains. Here, as in the neighboring Cuyamacas, you'll find hot summers, crisp autumns, snowy winters, and plenty of spring wildflowers. The drive itself is a pleasure, winding as it does along tree-lined country roads. Though most of Heise's land is in its natural state, there are campsites for tents and RVs, family picnic areas, and lovely hiking trails with views of the mountains and desert. Even on crowded weekends, the trails are nearly deserted; our tourist-to-trash estimate tells us that most people seem to prefer sitting around their campsites. On weekdays, it's very peaceful, and you should be able to get a good site without reservations. Call County Parks, 565-3600, for further information.

HISTORY:

For hundreds of years, Kumeyaay Indians came here in summer, staying to gather autumn acorns and leaving before the cold set in. After gold was discovered in Julian in the 1860s, the area provided lumber for the resulting building boom.

The park's original 200 acres were donated to the county in 1970 by William Heise, a German immigrant who had married well, made it big in the hearse business, and patented a number of offbeat inventions including, we are told, the pop-top trash can.

THE WALKS

Pick up a park map at the ranger station; it will give you some idea of how to find your way around. Remember you're in the mountains, well above 4000 feet, and the higher you are, the harder the walk. Just take it easy, and be prepared; carry water in summer, perhaps a small thermos of coffee or hot chocolate in winter. In winter, too, check on snow conditions before starting out. Year-round, wear shoes with good treads, since the paths are steep in places. A walking stick will help you pull yourself up the steep parts, as will the thought that uphill hiking is great aerobic exercise.

◆ Walk 1 The Cedar Trail

DISTANCE: 1.3 miles round trip. TIME: 45 minutes to 1 hour.

Park near the caravan area, not far from the entrance. A short paved service road leads southward through oaks, pines, and incense cedars, whose reddish wood is used in pencils. Just after you pass a pumphouse for the park's water, the dirt trail begins.

Frog pond, Cedar Trail

For an easier climb, and a very nice side trip, bear left at the signpost. Cross a wooden bridge over the usually dry creek, which could be a flowing stream in winter. One summer day, we ran into a plague of the legendary seven-year locusts here—cicadas, whose mature nymphs were emerging after years underground, sucking root juices and waiting for their chance at adult life. The males were humming all around us, trying to attract females—they sounded like high tension wires.

Meanwhile, every biting fly in the mountains was feasting on our legs, which made taking advantage of the log chairs facing the creekbed impossible. If you're here in early summer, you might consider bringing some insect repellant or wearing long pants. Unfortunately, we didn't.

Head up the stairs through bracken ferns, poison oak, and June-blooming wild roses, which smell even sweeter than they look. There's a second wooden bridge and, to the left, a pond. In summer, it's algae-covered, full of frogs and 3-inch tadpoles, and looks like the primordial soup. You can picture the whole process of evolution here, from the tiny

Time out on the trail

guppylike tadpoles; to the bigger ones with their first set of legs; to the frogs, newly amphibious, chirping; and finally to ourselves, the ultimate in land animals. At the edge of the water, we considered our roots, locking eyes with the tadpoles, wondering what they made of us.

We saw black-and-white dragonflies here, hovering over the pondweed, and an assortment of butterflies; it was our favorite spot on the Cedar Trail, though not really part of it.

When you're through at the frog pond, cross the bridge and walk uphill to the right. At the next signpost, bear left through the tall trees and poison oak. The path continues uphill and curves south at the park's property line.

Nearby, in spring and summer, you'll find patches of tiny wild strawberries and a number of white fairy lanterns. These lovely white flowers, also called globe lilies, do look like little Japanese lanterns and are one of our woodland favorites.

Keep going uphill and down, enjoying the pine-scented air. At just over a mile, there's a green expanse of bracken ferns. Soon you're at the pumphouse again, ready to take the path back to the caravan area.

◆ Walk 2 Canyon Oak Trail
DISTANCE: 3 miles round trip. TIME: 1.5 to 2 hours.

For a longer, more challenging trail, park near youth camp area 2 in the spaces marked "Parking for Hiking Trails," close to the restrooms. Walk uphill and turn right to reach the trailhead, across from site #86. Then follow the arrow 0.5 mile to the Canyon Oak Trail.

In spring and early summer, as you start uphill, look for 3-foot-tall bushes of woolly blue curls, a member of the mint family. The flowers— actually more purple than blue—have long, curling stamens.

The trail leads through oaks and pines, manzanita and mountain mahogany, and then alternates between woodlands and chaparral. Bear right at the first fork—it's less steep this way—and continue to a T crossing at about 0.3 mile. Again, go right; you'll soon be rewarded for your climb with your first mountain views.

Promptly at 0.5 mile, as the sign at the trailhead said, you'll see a signpost pointing left to the Canyon Oak Trail. Heading right leads on to the steeper Desert View Trail, which you might want to try someday.

This trail is steep enough for us, and pretty enough too. A word of caution though: the deerflies in early summer can be murder. Dressed in shorts, we punctuated our climb with colorful language, which didn't seem to disturb the flies at all.

Bear right at the next signpost and continue on, unless you're tired. If so, head down about 0.1 mile to the youth camp area and walk back to where we started. This would give you about a mile round trip.

There are rocks and fallen trees to rest on from time to time—just be sure you don't get your hindquarters into any poison oak. At the next signpost, at about 1.4 mile, a short uphill jog to the right will give you a little extra view. Continuing on a few hundred yards, you reach another signpost. Here, you can choose to go left to the Desert View Trail, a fairly steep, shadeless, but view-full 2-mile circuit.

This is usually as far as we go. We take the bypass trail right and then go right again. This is another good place to look for fairy lanterns in spring and early summer. Heading back, bear right at the signpost to catch that mountain vista again, and then continue left downhill. When you reach the fork, stay on the upper trail—remember, the other is steeper—till you're back at the parking area.

On weekdays, when it's quiet, you should have your choice of large, shady picnic tables. There's nothing like dining peacefully under the oak trees after the trail is done.

Cuyamaca Rancho State Park

◆

LOCATION:

Descanso/Cuyamaca. Take I-8 east to Highway 79 (Japatul Road). Turn left, go under the freeway, and, just after Descanso, turn left again onto Highway 79.

For Walk 1: Turn left on Viejas Boulevard and drive about 1 mile to the parking lot, just after Mizpah Road and before the Descanso Elementary School (TB405:D6).

For Walk 2: Follow Highway 79 north, passing Green Valley Falls Campground, to the park headquarters, 2 miles ahead on the right. Park near the old stone house about 0.2 mile in (TB405:E5).

HOURS:

Always open. The office at park headquarters is open on weekdays, 8:00 a.m. to 5:00 p.m.

DESCRIPTION:

This 30,000-acre wilderness park, just 40 miles from downtown San Diego, lies in the Cuyamaca Mountains, whose 6512-foot Cuyamaca Peak is the second highest point in the county (Hot Springs Mountain near Warner Springs is 21 feet higher). Here you can find dense pine and oak

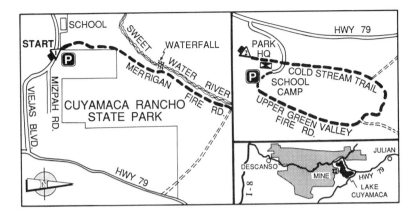

forests, broad alpine meadows, and 120 miles of hiking and riding trails. Mountain lions, bobcats, foxes, deer, and raccoons, and at least 100 species of birds make their homes here. Both Paso Picacho and Green Valley Falls campgrounds are excellent for camping or picnicking, with the latter having the advantage of a waterfall. For camping reservations, call 1-800-446-7275.

At park headquarters, there is a small museum of Indian history. Stop at the office for information brochures, books, and a detailed map of the park and campgrounds or ask to leaf through the photo album of local wildflowers, organized by color—a great aid to flower identification. You may also want to visit the old Stonewall Mine, a mile south of Lake Cuyamaca, where you can see an exhibit on the history of Southern California's richest gold mine. For additional information on any of the park's facilities, call 765-0755.

Another pleasant stop is Lake Cuyamaca itself. Though not part of the state park, it offers rental boats, good fishing, a new 3-mile trail around the lake, and picnicking. Group walks can be arranged by calling 447-8123 or 765-0515.

HISTORY:

For at least 7000 years, Kumeyaay Indians lived in this area they called Ah-ha-kwe-ah-mac, "the place where it rains." Spanish expeditions found them friendly, but determined to keep their independence. Far from the hub of mission activity, they managed to preserve their traditional lifestyle, continuing to spend summers in the mountains and winters in the desert or near the coast.

Inside the Indian Museum

In 1845, Governor Pio Pico gave Rancho Cuyamaca to Don Augustin Olvera, his niece's husband. Olvera was a prominent figure in Los Angeles politics, and the man for whom the main street of L.A.'s "Mexican quarter" was named.

In the 1860s, when gold was discovered near Julian, hundreds of prospectors and mine workers started pouring in, and the last of the local Indians were forced out and onto reservations.

In 1885, a dam was constructed at Lake Cuyamaca, a small sometime-lake the Spanish had called "the lake that dries up." Mountain water was brought down to the thirsty city of San Diego by a 35-mile redwood flume. By 1892, the gold rush was over, the Stonewall Mine having produced over $2 million in gold. The 20-year-old boom town of Cuyamaca survived for a few years as a summer resort and then disappeared.

In 1923, retired Beverly Hills businessman Ralph Dyar bought the rancho property to use for family vacations. Dyar built the stone house that is now park headquarters and enjoyed entertaining an assortment of movie stars and politicians at his mountain retreat. In 1933, he sold the property to the state for half its appraised value, with the proviso that it be kept open to the public forever.

◆ Walk 1 The Merrigan Fire Road

DISTANCE: 2 miles round trip. TIME: 1 hour.

Walk past the ranger residences, around the gate, and onto a wide sandy equestrian trail. Soon you'll be on the Merrigan Fire Road, following the upper part of the Sweetwater River, which flows from the mountains into San Diego Bay at Chula Vista. First, though, you have to cross an open meadow, passing live oaks, farmhouses, and probably, red-tailed hawks. After the meadow, continue on through chaparral and oak woodlands. In spring, there's lots of blue ceanothus blooming, along with the usual buckwheat and chamise; in summer, there's gold in these hills—golden yarrow, that is.

The path climbs much of the way, but gradually. You can't really see the Sweetwater River, but you can hear it, along with the squawks of ravens and, in summer, what Tennyson described, onomatopoetically, as the "murmuring of innumerable bees."

At about 0.75 mile, take the first left-forking path downhill for a nice surprise. Turn right again at the bottom, passing through wild roses, poison oak, and, in summer, yellow and white lotus, a member of the pea family. Just ahead is a delightful boulder-encircled pool and waterfall. The signs say "No Swimming," but you can soak your weary feet and stop for a picnic.

In spring, there are green mosses and lichens covering the rocks and ferns growing in the crevices of the boulders. In summer, there's lots of yellow monkey flower. Any time of year, you can watch the water striders skimming the surface and relax for awhile, enjoying the water music, even if you don't feel like picnicking. This is a fine place for reflective moments, and, except on summer weekends, you'll probably have it all to yourself.

A more adventurous way to reach this little oasis is to turn left at the bottom of the path, twice crossing the narrow river on stepping stones that seem to have been set out for that purpose. After the second crossing, just follow the sound of the waterfall. In winter, after rain, this path could be somewhat less practical.

Up at the main trail again, we turn around and head back, but you can continue on if you like. There are some pretty views, and good displays of spring and summer wildflowers, including showy purple penstemon, scarlet penstemon, and heliotrope phacelia, which looks like bushes of purple-headed caterpillars.

About 0.4 mile after the path to the waterfall, there's another turnoff, this one leading down to an old dam. Or stay on the road till, at 2 miles, it forks again, and goes down to the water. Many horseback riders cross here, and head toward the California Riding and Hiking Trail. The Merrigan Fire Road continues right to Highway 79.

◆ Walk 2 The Cold Stream Indian Trail

DISTANCE: 2 miles round trip. TIME: 1 to 1.5 hours.

This delightful trail starts just opposite the front door of the Cuyamaca Indian Museum. Walk down the steps and head north, along a leafy path shaded by tall Jeffrey pines and Kellogg oaks, the only one of our native oaks whose leaves change color and drop off in autumn. Its acorns, sweet and fat, were the Indians' favorite.

Jeffrey pines, whose pitch the Kumeyaay used as glue and whose seeds—pine nuts—were another favorite food, smell distinctly of vanilla. A group of botany students, whose professor had bragged he could always tell a Jeffrey pine by its scent, once sprinkled vanilla flavoring over a number of non-Jeffrey pines on the trail as a joke. The poor teacher was thoroughly confused. Try sniffing a tree trunk for yourself—it's a popular activity around here.

Small signs along the trail describe Indian life and plant usage. As you walk on, listen for the chatter of acorn woodpeckers and the "dee-dee-dee" of mountain chickadees. You may see Steller's jays carrying acorns off to some secret hiding place—so secret that they often forget where it is. These noisy blue jays are thought to be responsible for spreading oak trees throughout the west—the result of forgotten acorns taking root.

You'll soon cross the paved entrance road and pick up the path on the other side. The flat trail following Coldstream Creek takes you in and out of trees and open areas to the old Indian village site, where you can see two obvious grinding holes in the rock next to the sign.

At about 0.5 mile, you reach a broad meadow, with a good view of Stonewall Peak, named for Confederate general Stonewall Jackson. There's bird's nest thistle here, ground-hugging prickly plants whose green buds and, later, white flower clusters, look like eggs in a nest. Deer like to graze in the meadow; we've also seen bobcats and foxes slinking through the tall grasses.

Cuyamaca is one of the few places in San Diego County where there are still fields of native bunch grasses. Cattle brought here by the Spanish carried European grass seeds stuck in their hair, but even when these took root, they preferred the softer native grasses, and ate them up wherever they found them. The tougher imported grasses, like foxtail and the indigestible ripgut, took over.

In spring, look for the fuzzy gray-green plant called mule's ears—the leaves really do feel like a mule's soft ears. In late winter, they look rather lettuce-like; in spring, they grow taller, with showy yellow flowers. Here too are blue-eyed grass, purple vetch, pale blue wild iris, and magenta owl's clover, a parasite that attaches to the roots of other plants. As summer heat starts browning the meadows, you'll see bright patches of low-growing goldfields, which seem to have been splashed with gold paint.

Mountain meadow

At 0.7 mile, turn right and head back out of the meadow and up into the trees. We always feel better after hiking here, listening to the wind in the pines and breathing the clear unpolluted air. The path climbs gradually for a bit, and then descends. Take your time; there are plenty of rocks and stumps you can stop to picnic on, or just enjoy the scenery.

At about 1.2 miles, you'll come to the Upper Green Valley Fire Road. Turn right, and you're on your way back to park headquarters, passing the school camp, where urban sixth graders come to spend their annual week in the mountains. One day, as we were walking by the camp, we saw a mountain lion. Not the usual kind—this one was on a leash, being led around by a park ranger dressed up in a mountain quail suit, for the benefit of a TV crew. The big cat didn't seem to mind the camera, but the presence of the giant quail so unnerved him that he had to be put back in his trainer's van and soothed with a piece of pot roast. Actually, rangers tell us that there are many mountain lions in Cuyamaca Park—drawn by the herds of deer that live here.

Just before 2 miles, turn right at the fenced swimming pool and head up through the school camp and back to your car.

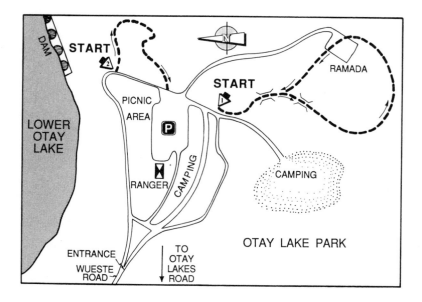

Otay Lake Park

◆

LOCATION:

Chula Vista. Take I-805 south to Telegraph Canyon Road, then head east 9 miles. Telegraph Canyon becomes Otay Lakes Road and intersects with Wueste Road. Take Wueste 3 miles south to the park entrance (TB407:E5).

HOURS:

The lake is open Wednesday, Saturday, and Sunday for fishing, boating, and, in summer, windsurfing. The park is open daily from 9:30 a.m. to sunset. $1.00 parking fee. *Note:* The park was temporarily closed in 1992 while repairs were made. Check before going there.

DESCRIPTION:

Otay is a city reservoir whose parkland is leased to the county and features ramada-shaded picnic areas, playgrounds, and a campground with individual and group sites. Some day in the not-too-distant future, the lake will be encircled by a new city, but for now, it's still unspoiled by development. The park is a good place for group picnics, short walks, and birdwatching. For camping and group picnic reservations, call County Parks, 565-3600. For information on fishing, boating, and wind-surfing, call City Lakes, 390-0222.

HISTORY:

This area has seen its share of climactic events. Nearby Otay Mesa was the site of the first controlled heavier-than-air flight in 1883. John Montgomery, for whom Montgomery Field in Kearny Mesa was named, flew his glider a full 600 feet, cruising 15 feet above the ground, 20 years before the Wright brothers' flight.

In 1916, rainmaker Charles Hatfield succeeded spectacularly in his attempt to end a drought. The original dam at Lower Otay burst, flooding the valley with 13 million gallons of water, washing houses out to sea and killing a number of people (see Lake Morena Park, p. 172). Construction of a new dam began later that year and was completed in 1919. Remains of the old dam can still be seen at the west side of the new one.

In 1957, the county leased 100 acres of land from the city and created the park and campground. Due to expire in 1989, the lease may not be renewed by the city, which may have development plans of its own. The facilities are somewhat run-down, awaiting a final decision.

THE WALKS

Drive in 3 miles to the parking lot near the ranger station, where swallows nest in the eaves.

◆ Walk 1 Border View Trail

DISTANCE: 1.2 miles round trip. TIME: 30 to 40 minutes.

Start behind the restrooms at the corner of the parking lot, where there's a "Self-Guided Nature Trail" sign. Walk down a few steps past wild oats, following the edge of the campground, in the shade of eucalyptus trees. On the tree trunks, look for rings of tiny holes made by red-breasted sapsuckers; you can see the gluey sap dripping from these bird-drilled "wells."

Whatever the season, there are lots of birds around. We saw black-and-white-striped Nuttall's woodpeckers, Anna's hummingbirds, red-shouldered hawks, cliff swallows, and a small, drab, but uncommon rock wren.

Cross a small bridge over a seasonal stream and continue on, bearing right down the steps, across a second bridge. The intermittent "whop-whop-whop" sounds overhead are made by bigger birds—navy helicopters from Ream Field, in Imperial Beach.

At about 0.5 mile is a clearing; to your right, you can see the Otay

Eucalyptus grove

water filtration plant. Bear left, toward a ruined water catchment, from which you can see, ahead and slightly to the right, the gun towers of recently built Otay Prison.

Bear left uphill, watching for kestrels and hawks soaring over the valley. At the top of the hill, surrounded by pepper trees, is a group camping area and playground. Looking westward from the ramada, you can see the white hangars of Brown Field, a private airfield just across the border from Tijuana Airport.

Pick up the trail again to the right—the women's side—of the restroom. Follow the rock-lined path downhill through spring-blooming horehound, a scentless member of the mint family, whose round clusters of tiny white flowers turn to dry pods in late summer.

Europeans brought horehound to America, and Americans brought it to California to use as a cold remedy. Horehound candies were the cough drops of yesteryear, though a lot of honey had to be added to mask the natural bitterness.

Cross a bridge of pipes farther down on the right and continue bearing right through the eucalyptus trees and back uphill to the parking lot.

◆ Walk 2 Dam View Trail

DISTANCE: 0.8 mile round trip. TIME: 30 minutes.

There are two "Nature Trail" signs opposite the playground; start at the one nearest the lake. Under a spreading eucalyptus about 0.2 mile in, there are cement benches where you can sit and admire the lake, the pinkish humps of the Jamul Mountains, and the rebuilt dam, dating from

1919, three years after the flood.

Entry to the dam is fenced off, but from time to time, you can watch adventurous types trying—and failing—to scale the fence.

If you see a ring of disturbed water with a green bubbling center out in front, to the left of the dam, that's where imported water is being pumped in. There are usually white terns and black cormorants sitting on the long strip of log boom that acts as a barrier to keep boats from getting too close to the dam.

For a good view of the whole dam thing, and the Otay River Valley, take a short walk downhill to your right, up to the cable fence. On the left side of the dam, you can see a jagged remnant of the original wall; to the right, on both sides of the cable fence, are some good-sized toyons, whose red berries are very noticeable in late fall.

Retracing your steps back to the concrete benches, look for raccoon tracks in the dirt—they look like the prints of a baby's hands. When you emerge from the detour, take the sort-of-steps uphill to your left. Bear right at the fork, continuing uphill. At the top is a wooden bench; behind you, to the southwest, are the distant hills of Tijuana.

Pass between the skinny stumps of three telephone poles and head back down to the playground and parking lot, bearing right toward the water.

Note: As you leave the park on Wueste Road, watch carefully for speeding traffic along Otay Lakes Road. It's a blind curve, and some of the locals seem to think it's a racetrack.

Potrero Park

LOCATION:

Potrero. Take Highway 94 east to Potrero. Go north 1 mile on Potrero Valley Road and east 1 mile on Potrero Park Road to the park entrance (TB408:E5).

HOURS:

9:00 a.m. to 5:00 p.m. $1.00 day-use fee. Overnight camping on weekends.

DESCRIPTION:

A county park way out in the country, Potrero has 115 acres of live oaks, grassy meadows, and good facilities for picnickers and campers.

There are ballfields, horseshoe pits, a playground, and a nature trail. For camping reservations, call County Parks, 565-3600.

HISTORY:

Before this area was inhabited, Indians used to bring their horses along a rough trail from Tecate, Mexico, to feed in the mountain meadows of Potrero, a Spanish word for "pasture land."

In 1868, one of San Diego's earliest port pilots, Captain C. G. McAlmond, took up residence here. He started a large family, and raised herds of cattle, pigs, and horses.

Mountain lions often preyed on errant livestock, and winter occasionally found valley residents knee-deep in snow. In 1916, Potrero felt the effects of the floods attributed to Hatfield the Rainmaker; 2 to 3 feet of water swamped the valley floor, and the roar of the dam collapsing at Otay, 20 miles away, could be clearly heard.

◆ The Walk

DISTANCE: 1 mile round trip. TIME: 30 minutes.

On the day we visited Potrero, the Society for Creative Anachronism was having a weekend campout. There were 700 people dressed in their versions of medieval costumes strolling through the park, some in full

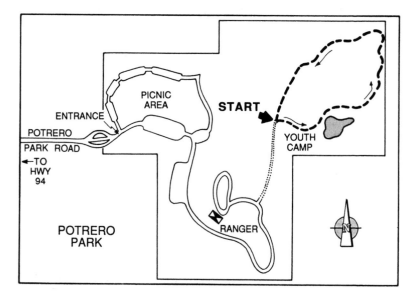

Young herpetologists

armor. It seems they gather here from time to time, and Potrero's broad fields are certainly a good place for jousting.

In our more contemporary garb, we found the trailhead (with some difficulty) by crossing the youth camp area at the northeast end of the campground and following the boundary fence north to the first left, an earthen dam across what was once a water-storage pond.

This really is a "self-guided nature trail;" you need to be alert to find it, and there are only a few markers on its whole 1-mile circuit. The first, on your right, identifies buckwheat, probably the most prevalent plant around.

Standing by the buckwheat, look down at the dead tree beside the dry pond bed; it's a popular perch for woodpeckers and other birds.

Just ahead on the left is another marker introducing you to Eastwood manzanita, which is taller than the coastal variety and has pretty pink flowers and larger berries.

After you cross the dam, take the path to the right. In late spring, you'll see the curly white flowers of salt heliotrope at your feet, and lots of yellow mustard on either side.

Also in spring, look for yellow monkey flower, the wildflower, not the bush. You'll see the foothills variety of bush monkey flower farther on; it's a pale apricot color.

There are several live oaks along the trail, though the next marker is at a scrub oak, about 0.3 mile from the trailhead. Not far away are some bird's foot ferns and the shiny, notched leaves of holly-leaf cherry.

The path you are following is actually a little streambed; in winter, you should see lots of mosses, lichens, and ferns here. In spring and early summer, there's golden yarrow, and the matted orange"witch's hair" of chaparral dodder.

Up a small hill just ahead, beside one of the large granite boulders that are prominent features of this part of the country, is a log bench. You might want to sit down for awhile and listen to the silence. (We, of course, heard distant shouting and sounds of swords and shields as medieval armies clashed on the field behind us.)

When you're ready to get back to the world, walk on through the chamise and the buckwheat. In late spring, keep an eye out for yellow mariposa lilies, whose wide "mouths" have silky hairs to trap pollen from insects' legs.

About 0.2 mile past the bench is another junction; bear right uphill and then downhill. On the right, just beyond the tall flat boulder, you may see springtime clumps of scarlet bugler. Bees love their tubular red blossoms.

Cross the smooth patch of granite and continue on to the wide dirt vehicle road ahead. From here, you can circle back to the youth camp where you started out, or head off to the picnic area for an oak-shaded barbecue.

Lake Morena Park

LOCATION:

Morena Village. Take I-8 east to Buckman Springs Road, go south 4 miles to Oak Drive, then west 3 miles to Lake Morena Drive and the park entrance (TB408:F4).

HOURS:

Half hour before sunrise to half hour after sunset. $2.00 day-use fee.

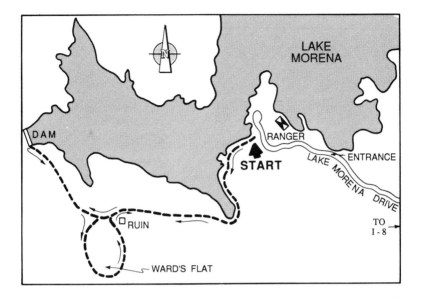

DESCRIPTION:

A 4500-acre recreational area surrounding a 1500-acre reservoir, Lake Morena Park is a popular spot for fishing, boating, windsurfing (summer only), or camping. The lake is stocked with big-time bass, catfish, and bluegill; fishermen need a state license and a daily permit. Rowboats and motorboats are available for rental on weekends. You can launch your own boat or sailboard for a small fee. There are two camping areas, on opposite sides of the lake, and facilities for group camping. Call County Parks, 565-3600, for information and reservations.

Besides the lake, there is a small museum at the ranger station, full of birds' nests, animal skulls and skins, old farm implements, and an odd collection of barbed wire. There are plenty of picnic tables and barbecues and, best of all, a wonderful, virtually unused trail that half-circles the lake and veers off through pine trees, meadows, and oak woodlands. All in all, a delightful place for dayhiking and feeling you're a million miles away from the crowds—even when the campgrounds are full.

HISTORY:

Centuries ago, Kumeyaay Indians camped in the valley that is now Lake Morena. The dam was built in 1902, but the reservoir was never really filled to capacity until January 1916. That's when the city council offered Los Angeles rainmaker Charles Hatfield $10,000 to fill the reservoir.

Hatfield, a sometime sewing machine salesman with a knack for attracting precipitation, set up his "evaporator towers" beside the dam and ended up filling not only the reservoir, but a good part of the county as well. In the downpour that followed, dams burst, bridges washed away, Mission Valley was flooded, and a number of hapless citizens were killed. The city refused to pay Hatfield unless he assumed liability, which he was understandably reluctant to do. He went on to other customers, was finally put out of business by the building of Hoover Dam, and took his rainmaking secrets to the grave. A Hollywood version of Hatfield's character can be seen in the movie "The Rainmaker," starring Burt Lancaster.

Three-quarters of a century later, Lake Morena faces a new set of water problems. The surrounding land is owned by the county, but the water is owned by the city, which, despite local protests, began lowering the level of the lake in late 1988, at the rate of 15 million gallons a day. City officials claimed that Lake Morena was too broad to store water efficiently and started sending the water to Otay Reservoir. A significant drop in water level here could seriously affect wildlife and make Lake Morena less attractive for recreational uses.

◆ The Walk

DISTANCE: 4 miles round trip (add 1 mile for Wards Flat meadow loop). TIME: 2.5 to 3 hours.

Drive in about 0.8 mile from the entrance and park just across from the closed service road, where our walk begins. There's a wonderful display of wildflowers along the trail in spring and early summer; we counted over 50 different kinds on one June day. We particularly enjoyed the blue ceanothus and the pink-fringed spine flower, a taller, more prickly cousin of Turkish rugging, and one of the less common members of the buckwheat family.

The lake is a lovely sight, ringed by mountains, dotted with small boats and, in summer, bright-colored windsurfer sails. Though it can get hot out here, the trail is pleasantly shaded by cottonwood trees; notice their heart-shaped leaves twinkling in the breeze—if there is a breeze. Notice, too, the live oaks, whose leaves are cupped to retain moisture. Keep an eye out for poison oak, which loves to twine itself around their trunks.

After you round the first good-sized cove, you'll see some Great Basin sagebrush, a pale gray-green variety of the more familiar California sagebrush, found along the coast. Our favorite flower on this trail, showy penstemon, blooms in late spring. It certainly is showy, with purple flower clusters on 3-foot stems. The blue delphinium you may see as the road starts climbing is pretty too, but somewhat less spectacular.

At just over a mile, there's a barbed-wire fence, which should be open. Not far ahead, the road forks; we like to take the right-hand path and head into the Coulter pines for a shady picnic. Just don't let any of the giant pine cones fall on your head; they're called "widow-makers" because their scales end in sharp, curved talons that could do some serious damage to your skull if you happen to be in the right place at the wrong time.

There's a large flat area here where you can spread out a blanket far enough from the trees to avoid the danger of becoming a conehead, and

Bobcat

close enough to appreciate the delicious piney smell.

Back on the main road, there's another fork just up ahead. To the left there's only a storage bin; bear right, passing an impressive ruin that was once a retreat for city officials. Built in the early 1920's, it was used for weekend R and R until it burned down 20 years later. The trees nearby are black locust, or false acacia; their fragrant white blossoms appear in June.

Again, the road forks; again, bear right. In spring, look for white-flowered common yarrow, which has a distinguished history. Achilles was said to have used its leaves to stop the flow of blood from the wounds of his soldiers—a kind of "Achilles' heal" that gives it its Latin name, *Achillea millefolium*. Early natives of California seem to have applied it to their own cuts and wounds, with equal success, but less notoriety.

If you're on the trail in early summer, don't forget to smell the roses—the wild roses—at about 1.8 miles. If you miss out on the roses, you can still admire the trees, like the oval-leaved Engelmann oaks, named for a 19th-century German botanist who was actually an expert on cacti.

Pretty soon, you'll start seeing the lake again. Notice the "ghost trees" in the water, with pale dead algae hanging from their branches. These trees were actually drowned when the water level was higher, and their roots and branches can be a real hazard to boaters, windsurfers, and fishermen.

You should see some wildlife as you're walking: a red-shouldered hawk flying over the lake, a mottled gopher snake slithering across the grounds, flashy red and blue dragonflies along the water's edge. Pass a metal storage shed and some power poles and continue uphill for a fine view of the dam and the mountains. Hold onto your hat! It can get windy here.

Follow the road downhill, as it curves past massive granite rocks and over to the dam. Look westward into the boulder-strewn valley—the result of dynamiting to build the dam. The dam itself would be a great place to sit and watch the sun go down, if you're camping at the lake. On a moonlit night, you might not even need a flashlight for the trip back.

The return trip is uphill, but not enough to make you pant, and generally shady. Our last time here, we had the unexpected bonus of seeing one of our favorite reptiles—the ring-necked snake, a small, slim, charcoal-colored snake with a red belly and a red neck band. When defending itself, this little snake coils its tail up into a knot and then, uncoiling rapidly, gives the startling effect of a big red, hungry mouth.

When you reach the main road again, take a left and head back the way you came, or go right through meadows and woodlands to the old group campsite at Ward's Flat, now returned to its natural state. This 1-mile loop is well worth the extra time; we love it.

You can picnic in the pines, where bright yellow orioles and black phainopeplas like to nest. It's so peaceful out here, you probably won't feel like rushing back. When you're ready, cross over the flat area to the east side of the meadow and head back along the vehicle road.

From this side, you get a good look at the rocky hillsides to the west, especially Morena Butte, a massive rock towering over the meadow. Look for raccoon, coyote, deer, horse, and bike tracks along the trail—they'll give you an idea of who's sharing the road with you.

At the triangular "057" sign, you reach the end of the loop and rejoin the main road again. Continue gently up and downhill for the rest of the trail.

If you're ready for another hike—not necessarily at this very moment—Lake Morena connects into the Pacific Crest Trail, which goes from the Mexican border all the way to Canada. The section here is more difficult and not as varied as the trail we've just taken, but if you're up for it, give yourself plenty of time and water—and enjoy! Look for the "PCT" sign near the park's entrance.

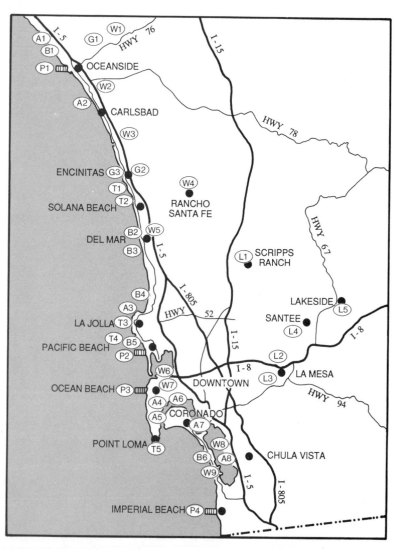

WALKING SHORTS

(A Bundle of Extras for More Walking Pleasure)

BEACHES
B1 • Harbor Beach
B2 • Fletcher Cove Park
B3 • North Torrey Pines Beach
B4 • Kellogg Park
B5 • Tourmaline Surfing Park
B6 • Silver Strand State Beach

TIDEPOOLS
T1 • Swami's Park
T2 • South Cardiff State Beach
T3 • South Coast Boulevard
T4 • False Point
T5 • Cabrillo National Monument

BAYSIDE AMBLES, SEASIDE STROLLS
A1 • Oceanside Harbor
A2 • Carlsbad Seawall
A3 • La Jolla Coast Walk
A4 • La Playa
A5 • Shelter Island
A6 • Harbor Island and Spanish Landing Park
A7 • Tidelands Park
A8 • J Street Marina

URBAN LAKES
L1 • Lake Miramar
L2 • Lake Murray
L3 • Chollas Lake
L4 • Santee Lakes
L5 • Lindo Lake

OCEAN PIERS
P1 • Oceanside Pier
P2 • Crystal Pier
P3 • Ocean Beach Pier
P4 • Imperial Beach Pier

SECRET GARDENS
G1 • Rosicrucian Fellowship Gardens
G2 • Quail Botanical Gardens
G3 • Self Realization Fellowship Gardens

WILD WINGS: A BIRDWATCHER'S GUIDE
W1 • Libby Lake
W2 • Buena Vista Lagoon
W3 • Batiquitos Lagoon
W4 • San Dieguito Reservoir
W5 • San Dieguito Lagoon
W6 • San Diego Flood Control Channel
W7 • Famosa Slough
W8 • Chula Vista Nature Interpretive Center
W9 • South Bay Biological Study Area

A whale's tail. Photo by George Zucconi courtesy of San Diego Natural History Museum

✦BY THE SHORES OF SAN DIEGO:
A BEACHCOMBER'S GUIDE✦

San Diego's greatest treasure is its beaches—76 miles of them, from the Orange County line to the Mexican border—and we all have our favorites. Families like La Jolla Shores and Coronado's Silver Strand; surfers like Trestles, north of Camp Pendleton, Swami's in Encinitas, the south end of Del Mar, and Windansea in La Jolla; singles head for Pacific Beach and Mission Beach.

In low tides, if you're feeling ambitious, and you don't mind getting your feet a *little* wet, you can actually walk all the way from Oceanside to the south end of La Jolla Shores, and from Coronado to the border. Check your tide tables, and plan to be back before the tide comes in.

Summer beaches are generally wider, sandier, flatter, and more crowded. In winter, storms can strip away as much as 15 feet of sand, exposing a surface of cobblestones which make walking more adventurous and won't be covered over again until summer. The damming of our rivers has kept sand from replenishing itself naturally and led to major problems with beach erosion, most recently in the winter storms of 1982–83.

But winter is really the best time for beachcombing. The storms that ravage our beaches wash up wonderful stuff to rummage through: perfect sand dollars, for example, those relatives of sea urchins and starfish, which, when alive, are covered with downy, purplish-gray spines that help them burrow down into the sand where they live.

And shells: knobby Kellett's whelks and wavy tops, nice 3-inch and 4-inch specimens, and light brown bubble shells, as well as the ubiquitous and often colorful scallop shells. Now and then, you can find a wavy top operculum, the protective trap door the living animal uses to seal up its shell, which looks like a wavy bit of shell itself.

Winter is also the time for tidepooling and whalewatching (see Exploring Tidepools, p. 189, and A Word About Whales, p. 186), but any time of year is fine for birdwatching. At the water's edge, you can usually see sandpipers and sanderlings scurrying about on quick little feet and lazier sea gulls hoping for a handout. Overhead, there are often flocks of pelicans flying in a rough V-formation, searching the waves for schools of anchovies, their favorite food.

Kids and kelp. Photo by Barbara Moore

Sometimes there are pods of playful dolphins surfing just offshore. Don't mistake them for sharks just because you see their dorsal fins; these large gray animals are intelligent mammals, and not at all dangerous. A more common hazard than sharks is stingrays, which lie invisibly on the ocean floor and can perforate your foot if you step on them. It's always a good idea to shuffle your feet when you walk into the water so they know you're coming and can get out of the way.

Another of our favorite local marine mammals is the California sea lion, seen occasionally swimming near the surf line or resting on a rock. Just south of the Children's Pool in La Jolla, you can usually find quite a few of them, along with harbor seals, basking in the sun on what is called—though they share it with sea birds—Seal Rock.

If you want to tell the seals from the sea lions, harbor seals have rounder heads and no ear flaps; their short front flippers look like paws. Sea lions have more doglike faces and long front flippers; by folding their back flippers under their bodies, they can "walk" on land. Sea World's performing seals are actually California sea lions.

You may see round translucent blobs of jellyfish washed up on the sand; even when dead, they can still sting, so don't pick one up to examine it. Kelp is another beach phenomenon; odd lengths of these large brown algae frequently break off from our offshore kelp forests. You'll most likely notice three kinds: 150-foot-long strands of giant kelp, with large ridged "leaves" and small, pear-shaped floats that pop when you step on them; feather boa kelp, which looks just like its name; and bull kelp, with a single melon-sized float and a long, leafless strand that makes a perfect beach jump-rope.

The algin found in kelp is used in a staggering variety of products, including chocolate syrup, toothpaste, beer foam, ketchup, finger paints, floor wax, hand lotions and cosmetics. Kelco, a local company, regularly harvests the prolific giant kelp, which can grow as much as 2 feet a day. Kelp is 92 percent water, so harvesting must be done on a large scale, but cutting the top few feet off the kelp canopy encourages replacement growth.

If you happen to be in the right place at the right time, you may get to witness the spectacular late-night spawning of hundreds of tiny grunion (see A Word About Grunion, p. 185). But even if you miss the grunion, there's always the human carnival of surfers, beach bunnies, fishermen, kayakers, joggers, and just plain folks who frequent our beaches every day.

Here are a few of our favorite spots, and their main attractions.

Harbor Beach

LOCATION:

Oceanside. Parking near Harbor Drive South (TB9:B5).

DESCRIPTION:

Heavily de-sanded by storms and the building of the harbor, much of this wide beach's white sand was brought in by truck. Walk south, skirting the mouth of the San Luis Rey River to the Oceanside Pier, or beyond. The paved promenade along the Strand from 9th Street to Wisconsin is especially good for wheelchairs.

Fletcher Cove Park

LOCATION:

Solana Beach. Parking at the end of Plaza Street (TB29:C5).

DESCRIPTION:

In the 1920s, Solana Beach developer Ed Fletcher used hydraulic water pressure to cut an opening from the bluffs to the sea, so residents of his community could have an ocean view. Walk north to the tidepools at Cardiff's Table Tops reef, or south to the San Dieguito River in Del Mar, where a path leads up to tiny, bluff-top Woodward Park, where the remains of 10,000-year-old Del Mar Man were found in 1929. From here, there's a 360-degree view of the coastline, racetrack, and, in winter, migrating gray whales. The north strip of beach can be nonexistent in high tides; check your tide tables before setting out.

North Torrey Pines Beach

LOCATION:

Del Mar. Parking along North Torrey Pines Road or in the large parking area (fee in summer) off Carmel Valley Road (TB34:A5).

DESCRIPTION:

A popular family beach, good for swimming and boogie boarding. Walk north to the river mouth in Del Mar, passing tidepools and the remains of an old public pool built to keep swimmers and stingrays—"the dread stingarees"—apart. Look for sun-bleached sand dollars along the way. Walk south for impressive sandstone bluffs with 50-million-year-old fossil oysters, clams, and snails embedded in them. In low tides, continue on to Black's Beach and La Jolla Shores. You can vary the return by detouring through Torrey Pines Reserve, taking the steps just north of Flat Rock.

Kellogg Park

LOCATION:

La Jolla Shores. Parking in the lot off Camino del Oro (TB44:A3).

DESCRIPTION:

Good swimming and boogie boarding; crowded in summer. There's a grassy picnic area and a short paved promenade, good for wheelchairs. To the north are Scripps Pier—you can detour to the Aquarium—and the tidepools at Dike Rock. To the south are more tidepools, just below the Marine Room. This beach is a favorite of scuba divers, who explore the kelp forests of its offshore underwater reserve.

A WORD ABOUT GRUNION

Do you believe in grunion? They do exist, even if you've never seen them, and every year, in spring and summer, they come up on our sandy beaches for an amazing, all-out spawning spree.

Around midnight, just after high tide on the nights following a new or full moon, thousands of these 6-inch silvery fish start making their way ashore—somewhere.

Stranded on the sand, the female digs in below the surface to deposit her eggs, while the male wraps himself around her to fertilize them. It's a live fish sex show, and you'd be very lucky to see it.

When their spawning is over, the grunion are ready to catch the next wave back to sea, unless prevented by frantic humans splashing through the shallow surf, armed with flashlights and buckets, trying to scoop up the wet wriggling bodies with their bare hands. This is the only legal way to catch grunion, and you still need a California fishing license. If you do happen to get your hands on a bucketful, grunion are delicious dipped whole in flour or cornmeal and fried—except in April and May, when they're protected by law, and can only be observed.

Whatever month you choose, it's anybody's guess whether the grunion will show up on a particular beach or a particular night, so warm clothes, a hot thermos, and a philosophical attitude are definitely in order.

Local tide tables will give you the dates and times of predicted runs, but there are no guarantees. Only the grunion know when and where they are actually coming ashore.

Tourmaline Surfing Park

LOCATION:

Pacific Beach. Parking at the end of Tourmaline, off La Jolla Boulevard. (TB43A:F6).

DESCRIPTION:

Look for fossil scallops in the bluffs just south of the parking lot. Walk north past tidepools to False Point, south to Crystal Pier or all the way to the Mission Beach jetty. Plenty of action on the P.B. boardwalk.

Silver Strand State Beach

◆

LOCATION:

Coronado. Parking in the lots off the Silver Strand, Highway 75 (fee in summer) (TB70Z:E1).

DESCRIPTION:

Wide, sandy family beach, usually uncrowded. Walk north to the Hotel Del or south to the Imperial Beach Pier. Good winter shelling.

——— A WORD ABOUT WHALES ———

Every winter, thousands of California gray whales pass by our beaches on their annual southward migration. When the storm season begins in the icy Bering Sea, these massive mammals head for the warm lagoons of Baja California, where they mate, calve, and rest for awhile before starting the long trip back in the spring.

Pregnant females leave first, then courting trios—a female and two randy males. Females are kept very busy during breeding season, entertaining male after male on migration and in the calving lagoons, where occasionally newborns are squashed by the amorous activity. It was previously thought that one of the males helped the other get into position, and kept him in place. But as naturalists have recently pointed out, there are no known animals that need help with their coupling.

Last to join the migration are the one- and two-year-olds, still sexually immature. Some never make it all the way to Baja, preferring instead to dawdle along the California coast.

On the southern leg of the journey, the whales swim close to shore, following coastal landmarks, and sometimes poking their heads up for a quick look around, a behavior called "spyhopping." More often you'll see a spout—the whale's exhalation of air and water. If you're very lucky, you'll see a whale "breaching"—hurling its bus-sized body out of the water. Some scientists think this could be a kind of "jumping for joy."

It's a long trip, and gray whales are not built for speed. Moving along at 4 or 5 miles an hour, it takes them about three months to cover the 5000 miles to Baja.

Because they swim so slowly, white star-shaped whale barnacles are able to attach themselves to the whale's blue-black skin, giving it a grayish appearance. Orange whale lice also ▶▶▶

▶▶▶ come along for the ride, settling in near the blowholes. Seen up close, the whale's body is a mottled mass of parasites.

Winter whalewatching cruises give you a chance to get a good look at the California grays. Scripps Aquarium and the Museum of Natural History offer naturalist-led weekend trips in January and February. If you can't make one of those, there are a number of sportfishing outfits in Mission Bay, San Diego Bay, and Oceanside that offer daily cruises. Just look in the Yellow Pages under "Fishing Parties" and choose the most convenient. Reservations are a must, and so is warm clothing; it can get cold and damp out there while you're waiting to see a spout.

For landlubbers, there are good vantage points at the Carlsbad Seawall, Swami's Park in Encinitas, Seagrove and Powerhouse Parks in Del Mar, Torrey Pines Reserve, Coast Boulevard in La Jolla, Cabrillo National Monument in Point Loma, and Border Field State Park in Imperial Beach. Piers and beaches are also good places for whalewatching, though in recent years, whales have been staying farther offshore, probably to avoid all those whalewatching boats. During migration season, Cabrillo offers daily whale talks and films—call 557-5450 for details.

More about whales:

• All whales are descended from the same primitive hooved animals as cows, goats, and sheep.

• About half a gray's weight is fat, or blubber. A 6-inch layer keeps them warm in the Arctic and gives them energy for their long journey. During the eight months away from their home waters, they eat little or nothing, saving themselves for summer gorging.

• Gray whales may weigh as much as 40 tons and grow as long as 50 feet, but they can't swallow anything big; their esophagus is only the size of a baseball. They live off some of the smallest creatures in the ocean—tiny shrimplike amphipods, or krill—but they can put away a ton or two of these a day.

• Gray whales have no teeth; instead they have baleen, a set of fringed plates that look like hemp curtains and work to filter out mud and seawater and trap food inside their mouths. Whalebone, once found in combs, umbrella spokes, and ladies' corsets, is actually baleen. The expression "I'm going to whale the daylights out of you" came from the use of whalebone for buggy whips.

• A gray's gestation time is about 13 months. The newborn calf is 14 to 15 feet long and weighs 1500 to 2000 pounds—about the size of a compact car. It can consume 50 gallons of its mother's milk every day, and gain 2 or 3 pounds an hour! Whale milk is about 40 percent fat, really more like whipped cream.

Beachwalkers

⋆EXPLORING TIDEPOOLS⋆

If you don't mind getting your feet wet, walking slowly, bending down a lot, and leaving no stones unturned, tidepools are something you should definitely look into. Generally speaking, there are two high and two low tides every day, with the highest and lowest occurring at the time of the new or full moon. Low, or *minus,* tides expose the rocky reefs along our shores, giving us a look at many marine animals we never get to see outside of an aquarium.

Tidepooling is free, fascinating, and addictive, especially in winter, when minus tides tend to come at convenient afternoon hours. It's best to go out when the tide is still receding, about an hour before low tide, so you'll have plenty of time to explore; pick up a tide table at your local lifeguard station, bait-and-tackle shop, or surf shop, and plan ahead. New Year's Day usually has a good low tide, and tidepooling is one of our favorite ways to start off the year.

Start at the Spray Zone, reached only by the highest tides. Here are tiny black periwinkle snails, volcano-shaped buckshot barnacles, and insectlike isopods, which will actually drown if immersed in water.

In the lower High Tide Zone, covered and uncovered by water every day, you'll see blue-black mussels, attached to rocks and each other by byssus fibers, used in the Mediterranean in ancient times to make cloth of gold. There are hundreds of green anemones here, animals that look more like flowers.

Touch one gently near its mouth center and it will close around your finger, expecting lunch. Smaller prey than we are paralyzed by the poison darts in the greenish tentacles, and sucked into the anemone's stomach. All we feel is a faint stickiness, not at all unpleasant.

On your way to the Mid-Tide Zone, hermit crabs will probably catch your eye as they scurry about in their borrowed seashells, looking for food. The snails who were the shells' original occupants moved a lot slower, and ended up in the bellies of voracious sea stars—starfish—who spit out the shells when they finished eating.

Clinging to the rocks are limpets and armor-plated chitons; under ledges, look for honey-combed colonies of sandcastle worms.

The Low Tide Zone, exposed on minus tide days, is where most of the really exciting stuff is. Here, in the shallow pools, are spidery brittle stars, spiny sea urchins, wavy top snails, the large brown shell-less snails

called sea hares, which can grow up to 35 pounds, and even a few shy octopuses. There are red and orange bat stars too, though pollution and
warmer water seem to have depleted their numbers.

Most of these animals are not in plain view, but have to be uncovered. A whole world can be found by turning over a rock, but don't
forget to replace the rock when you're through looking or the animals
won't survive your visit.

Resist the temptation to take anything home with you; our local

Tidepools at Cabrillo

marine life is protected. We like to carry clear plastic cups to keep interesting specimens in sea water while we observe them face to face. If you do the same, be sure to put everything back where you found it, and *don't* leave your cup on the beach.

Serious tidepoolers come prepared for a wet walk. Wear old tennis shoes that still have some tread to them and shorts or long pants you can roll up. Try leaving a dry pair of shoes and socks in the car to change into; after an hour or two of tidepooling, there's nothing like the joy of warm feet. On winter days, a thermos of something hot is welcome too.

If you're ready to tidepool, here are some of San Diego's best sites.

Swami's Park

LOCATION:

Encinitas, just south of the Self Realization Fellowship on Highway 101. Limited parking in the lot, or park on the street (TB24:D6).

DESCRIPTION:

A small grassy park above a popular surfing beach, Swami's is named for Swami Yogananda, founder of S.R.F. (see Self Realization Fellowship Meditation Gardens, p. 217). There are restrooms, picnic tables, and 127 steps going down to the beach. North of the steps, there's nearly a mile of reef, where you can find sea hares, brittle stars, bat stars, octopuses, and an occasional seal.

South Cardiff State Beach

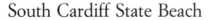

LOCATION:

Solana Beach, south of Restaurant Row in Cardiff. Easy access and lots of parking (TB29:B4).

DESCRIPTION:

A good place to take children. South of the parking lot, there's 0.25 mile of reef with lots of hermit crabs, sea hares, crabs, anemones.

South Coast Boulevard

◆

LOCATION:

La Jolla, south of Cuvier Street (TB43A:E2).

DESCRIPTION:

Smooth sandstone rocks and small sandy coves. Dark algae-covered patches are slippery when exposed. Heading south, there's 0.5 mile of reef, with deep, narrow channels, where garibaldi, opal eye, and sea hares graze.

False Point

◆

LOCATION:

Between Bird Rock and Pacific Beach. Access on Sea Ridge Drive and Linda Way, off La Jolla Boulevard (TB43A:F6).

DESCRIPTION:

Steps down to the rocky shore, some rock scrambling. About 1.5 miles of reef. Sea urchins, hermit crabs, abalones, and nudibranchs.

Cabrillo National Monument

◆

LOCATION:

Point Loma. No parking fee in lower tidepool area (TB64:B6).

DESCRIPTION:

About 1 mile of reef to explore. Best finds are around the point, about 0.5 mile in. Large chitons, whelks, colorful nudibranchs, and giant sea hares. Ranger-led tidepool walks (see Cabrillo National Monument, p. 70).

Sea-sculpted sandstone. Photo by Barbara Moore

Leave nothing but footprints...

◆ BAYSIDE AMBLES, SEASIDE STROLLS ◆

Oceanside Harbor

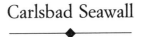

LOCATION:

Oceanside, Harbor Drive (TB9:B4).

DESCRIPTION:

A 2-mile paved path circles around from the Villa Marina Hotel to South Harbor Drive, passing sailboats, shops, restaurants, and an assortment of gulls and pelicans along the way. There's ample free parking, except near the beach at the south end, where parking costs $2.00 and there are restrooms, ramadas, picnic tables, and a playground.

Walk on the beach or the jetties, or stroll around the marina—a nice, flat place to ride bikes too. In winter, whalewatching cruises leave from Helgren's Sportfishing.

Carlsbad Seawall

LOCATION:

Carlsbad Boulevard near Ocean Street (TB13:F5).

DESCRIPTION:

The Great Wall of Carlsbad is a corridor of sand-colored concrete between the bluffs and the beach, and a good place for a paved beach walk, as long as you're tall enough to see over the 4-foot wall.

This is actually an erosion control project, designed to keep the bluffs from crumbling down. It's a good place to see some of the sand-dune plants that beachfront development has been bulldozing away.

From spring through fall, look for the magenta flowers of sand verbena, trailing its oval-leafed vines down the bluffs. There's sea rocket too, a white-flowered relative of wild radish, and yellow beach lotus, a member of the pea family.

Probably easiest to recognize is statice, popular with bees and florists; its long-stemmed purple flowers rise from a clump of large, curly leaves.

There are patches of bright green New Zealand spinach, with its small, spade-shaped leaves, and usually lots of tumbleweed, that typical western plant that's really an immigrant—Russian thistle—with appropriately red stems, and red-tinged white flowers. As it ages, tumbleweed turns into a dry, spiny mass that blows in the wind, scattering thousands of seeds as it tumbles along.

The seawall is a fine place for watching shorebirds, dolphins, whales, surfers, and sunsets, and can be pretty exciting in high tides, with the waves splashing against it.

The city of Carlsbad recently put in a pedestrian path along the overlooking stretch of Carlsbad Boulevard, so you can take the high road one way and the low road to return, for a distance of about 1.25 miles.

La Jolla Coast Walk

LOCATION:

Torrey Pines Road at Coast Walk, a small street between La Jolla Shores and Prospect (TB43A:F1).

DESCRIPTION:

This beautiful half-hour cliffside walk is a little hard to find the first time, but once you've found it, you won't be sorry. There are spectacular views of the ocean, La Jolla Shores, and the bluffs of Torrey Pines and the North Coast; on a clear day, you can see all the way to the Encina Power Plant in Carlsbad.

Parking is the biggest problem. There are a few spaces near the "Ecological Preserve" signs and about 0.1 mile farther in, but these are often taken. Parking at the southern end, near the Shell Shop in La Jolla, is even more difficult; you may want to try starting from whatever spot you can find on Coast Boulevard.

Alternatively, you can park at La Jolla Shores and walk down the beach as far as the Marine Room, where you can cut up to Spindrift Drive, which becomes Princess Street. Turn right onto noisy Torrey Pines, and continue south about 0.3 mile to the walk's beginning.

Whatever way you get there, you'll be strolling between the villas and the deep blue sea, with benches along the way so you can sit and admire the view. Just keep following the trail along the cliff's edge to the grove of

Torrey pines above the Sunny Jim Cave, where bootleggers reportedly stashed their liquor during Prohibition.

La Playa

LOCATION:

Point Loma. Park on Talbot Street and Anchorage Lane, near the San Diego Yacht Club (TB64:C1).

DESCRIPTION:

La Playa—"the beach"—is Point Loma's best-kept secret, a lovely 0.5-mile stretch of shoreline between two yacht clubs, passing some of the best-kept lawns and stateliest homes in San Diego. There's a real Mediterranean feel to the view southward—a green hill (loma means "hill") covered with red-roofed houses, looking down on the picture-pretty cove with its rows of silvery masts.

A century and a half ago, hides were tanned and beef fat melted down into tallow on these shores, waiting for tall ships to carry them away. Then, the area was known as Hide Park. Today, the occasional sunbather dozes on a beach towel by the water, her ship having already come in, and you see the kind of lush subtropical plantings that used to be found only in Hawaii.

This path is popular with lunchtime walkers from the nearby Naval Ocean Systems Center. It comes out to the street just past tiny La Playa Yacht Club, but you can continue on along San Antonio, about four and a half short blocks.

On the corner of San Antonio and Owen, there's a huge, fantastic pink-barked eucalyptus spreading across the street—a favorite daytime perch for night herons. At Kellogg Street, you're back on the playa again, with another 0.25 mile of quiet beach ahead. Here, you can inspect the bayside rocks for scurrying shore crabs and look across the channel to Shelter Island.

Shelter Island Bayside Walk

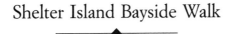

LOCATION:

San Diego. Take Rosecrans to Shelter Island Drive. Park at the circle where the road ends, near the Friendship Bell tower and the Harbor Police (TB64:C2).

Tunamen's Memorial

DESCRIPTION:

Shelter Island was born in the 1950s after wartime dredging deepened the bay for navy ships and heaped up enough mud to create a pleasure island of hotels, restaurants, and yacht clubs, connected to the mainland by a causeway.

Near the flagpole, just south of the Harbor Police building, you can sit and watch boats going by, and admire the homes of Point Loma's La Playa section across the channel. Also across the channel are the cement block building of the Naval Ocean Systems Center, and the docks of the Nimitz Marine Facility of Scripps Institution of Oceanography. If any of Scripps' research vessels are in town, this is where you'll find them.

If you have good eyes, you can see the caged sea lions, used by the navy for deep-water research. You can hear their barking—the sea lions', not the navy's—when the wind is right. To the south is the entrance to San Diego Bay, where you'll often see big ships coming in. It can get pretty windy out here, but otherwise it's a wonderful place to pass an hour or two, with convenient picnic tables, benches, restrooms, and even telephones along the promenade.

Start your walk with a look at the Friendship Bell, presented to San Diego by the citizens of Yokohama, Japan. Ducks, coots, gulls, and pigeons love to congregate around the surrounding pool and grassy area.

At about 0.3 mile is the bronze Tunamen's Memorial, surrounded by thorny natal plums, with sweet-smelling, jasmine-like flowers and round red fruits. Notice how it takes three men to hook one tuna, as it did before the huge nets called tuna seines revolutionized tuna fishing. San Diego was once America's tuna capital until the decreasing tuna population, foreign imports, and stringent U.S. laws protecting dolphins accidentally caught in the seines led to the canneries' closing and the industry's decline.

A 0.5-mile stroll will bring you to the Shelter Island Fishing Pier, where you can usually get a good, close look at some of our local pelicans that like to perch on the pier or the low roof of the snack bar, hoping for a handout. In the 1970s, these big-billed birds with 6-foot wingspans were considered an endangered species. Toxic residues of DDT in the fish they ate had led to a thinning of their eggshells; eggs were often too fragile to survive the parent's weight during incubation. More recently, pelicans seem to have made a remarkable recovery, managing to adapt and survive like the rest of us.

Another 0.5 mile brings you to the boat launch area near the Bali Hai Hotel, a logical turnaround point.

Harbor Island Drive and Spanish Landing Park

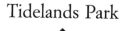

LOCATION:

San Diego, south of Lindbergh Field (TB59:E6).

DESCRIPTION:

Close to the airport, Harbor Island isn't quite as peaceful as its landfill twin, Shelter Island, but it's still a good place for bayside walks.

At Harbor Island Drive, park near Tom Ham's Restaurant at the west end. As you walk along the paved promenade, you'll be looking across at the hangars and installations of North Island, San Diego's naval air base, and moving toward the downtown skyline and the Coronado Bay Bridge.

Here in the bay, you can see aircraft carriers and destroyers, tuna seiners, cruise ships, and freighters, mixing in with the small pleasure boats of weekend—and weekday—sailors.

There are benches along the way, restrooms, and some green grass to soften the concrete ribbon. A good turnaround point is the parking lot at the Reuben E. Lee; if you get this far, you'll have come about 1.5 miles.

At Spanish Landing Park, where Vizcaino is said to have landed in 1602, start your walk at the lot at the west end of Harbor Drive, across from the Naval Training Center. From here, you can see the small boats and large hotels of Harbor Island. There are grassy areas, occasional benches, restrooms, and bike racks too; unlike Harbor Island Drive, Spanish Landing is open to cyclists.

It's about 1.5 miles to the turnaround at the east end, or you can head south and continue around, connecting into Harbor Island Drive.

Tidelands Park

LOCATION:

Coronado, first right turn after crossing the bridge (TB65:C4).

DESCRIPTION:

A pleasant park in the shadow of the Bay Bridge, with broad grassy areas, a small sandy beach, playgrounds, and a sweeping view of the bay, the bridge, and downtown San Diego, Tidelands is a good spot for a short paved walk, a picnic, or a 1-mile bike circuit. Someday, the path here will connect into the Bay Route Bikeway that goes along the Silver Strand. For now, enjoy the park for itself, and watch for kingfishers, herons, and other waterbirds; they seem to like it here too.

J Street Marina
(Bayside Park and Chula Vista Launching Ramp)

LOCATION:

Chula Vista, between J and G Streets, off Marina Parkway (TB69:B5).

DESCRIPTION:

Bayside Park, across from Rohr Industries, is a pretty city park with green grass, bay views, picnic tables, a paved jogging/walking/biking/skating path, restrooms, and a concession. Walking out on the cement pier, you can see Imperial Beach, Mexico, and the smoking San Diego Gas and Electric power plant. Walking back, there's the nicer sight of downtown San Diego, framed by the Coronado Bridge.

You can watch the fishermen trying their luck in the bay, where it's probably luckier *not* to catch anything, since it's the most polluted on the West Coast. As on all public ocean piers, no fishing license is required.

A stroll through Bayside Park takes you past an RV resort and marina where you can admire the boats and feed the ducks—you can even buy duck food at the concession.

Half a mile south is the Chula Vista Launching Ramp, whose marshy south side is a good place to birdwatch. Park in the first lot, just across from the power plant; to the right of the rounded storage tanks, look for the great salt pyramids of the Western Salt Company. Many shorebirds visit the mudflats here at low tide; migrating ducks come here in winter. Walk around the perimeter, with grass, picnic tables, and benches along the way.

Hottentot fig, a.k.a. ice plant

◆ URBAN LAKES ◆

Lake Miramar

◆

LOCATION:

Scripps Ranch, entrance on Scripps Lake Drive (TB40:C2). The lake is open Saturday through Tuesday, sunrise to sunset, except for 3 weeks in October. Walkers can come in every day; just park outside on the street.

DESCRIPTION:

A city reservoir popular with fishermen and picnickers, Lake Miramar has several picnic areas, a concession, and a boat dock where you can rent a boat or launch your own. For reservations, call 390-0222.

As on all city lakes, fishermen need both state and daily permits, available at the concession. In summer, the lake is open to sailboarders. There are restrooms near the entrance, and portapotties strategically located along the paved lake road.

The area here was once part of Rancho Miramar, the 4000-acre retreat of newspaper tycoon E. W. Scripps, whose older half-sister, the reclusive Ellen Browning Scripps, became San Diego's leading philanthropist. Across the street from the entrance, beyond the fenced-in pond, you can see the remains of a stone wall on the property where E. W.'s daughter Nackey lived for many years. Her husband, Tom Meanley, had been Scripps' secretary. When the two eloped in 1916, the old man was infuriated, but he still left them a fine piece of real estate, which their heirs sold in 1985 for $11 million.

Park in the small dirt parking area just left of the exit road and take the paved path heading west toward the dam. Don't be put off by the "Keep Moving" sign—it's for fishermen, who aren't supposed to fish beyond the gate.

This is one of the few dams in the county that people are allowed to walk across. High above Mira Mesa, you can look westward to Mt. Soledad in La Jolla and, on clear days, the Pacific Ocean. Here, where no cars are allowed, you'll usually find other walkers, joggers, skaters, and cyclists sharing the road with you.

Notice the cormorants, pelicans, and gulls resting on the water tower in the lake. Cormorants and pelicans dive for fish, and the gulls try to steal the fish from them. In spring and summer, there are families of mallards and coots swimming in and out of the cattails. In winter, you'll see long-necked western grebes and black-and-white lesser scaup. Rangers tell us that bobcats and coyotes come out of the hills at night to feed on the waterbirds.

At about 0.5 mile, on the north side of the dam, the road turns east and continues another 0.75 mile until it joins the vehicle road. Here are many of the usual chaparral plants—chamise, monkey flower, manzanita, golden yarrow, black sage, and scrub oak. In late spring, the north slopes are covered with bright magenta canchalagua. On the hilltops across the lake is the newer growth typical of the area—pink and gray housing developments.

This is where we turn around and head back. But you can continue another 4 miles around the lake on the vehicle road, stopping at one of the picnic areas for lunch.

Lake Murray

LOCATION:

La Mesa, entrance on Kiowa Drive (TB55:B6). Use alternate entrances at Murray Park Drive and Baltimore Drive on Monday and Tuesday, when the Kiowa Drive gates are closed.

DESCRIPTION:

Lake Murray, located in the most developed section of Mission Trails Regional Park, is a city reservoir with ducks to feed, birds to watch, and a paved shoreline trail to follow. The trail, more of a road really, is a fairly flat 3.5 miles each way, and is popular with joggers, fitness walkers, and bike riders. It's especially pleasant on wheels; kids might want to try it on skateboards or skates.

On the southeast side of the lake, not far from the entrance, are picnic tables, barbecues, and restrooms. Fishing is permitted on weekends and holidays from mid-March to the end of October. A valid state license and day permit are required.

At this time, boating is allowed on the lake on Wednesday, Saturday, and Sunday. Bring your own boat or rent one; call 390-0222 for reservations.

Once part of the nearly 60,000 acres of grazing lands owned by the San Diego Mission, this was the site of La Mesa Dam, built in 1895, and now buried beneath the waters of Lake Murray. The present dam was built in 1918, and extended in 1953. For 12 years, the lake was closed to the public because of an infestation of hydrilla, an annoying weed that clogs irrigation canals, spoils water quality, snags hooks and lures, and winds around boat propellers. It was reopened in the spring of 1987.

The lake circuit is not a particularly "wild" walk—almost everything here was recently planted and is carefully maintained—but you can see a number of birds, and it's a pretty spot, even if it is a bit suburban. In winter, hundreds of gulls have taken to visiting here. In spring, the soft cooing of mourning doves will accompany you as you walk. If you're lucky, you might see a roadrunner dart out in front of you; keep an eye out for rabbits and lizards too.

In spring, the area is bright with yellow Caltrans daisies and mustard. You'll appreciate the occasional shade of a pepper or eucalyptus tree, since it can get pretty warm here on a sunny day, especially when you're walking on asphalt.

There's plenty of chaparral broom, sagebrush, prickly pear, and some castor bean trees, with a few ornamentals like coral and silk oak trees planted in between. On the northeast side, you'll find yourself practically in people's backyards, as you head towards Cowles Mountain, the highest point in the city, once used by Indians as a solstice observation site.

At the 1.5-mile marker, the road turns west. To your right, behind fencing, is a golf course; watch out for stray balls. If you go all the way, there are two eucalyptus groves near the end of the road that would make good rest stops before heading back.

Chollas Lake

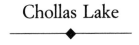

LOCATION:

College Grove. The park entrance is at 6350 College Grove Drive (TB61:F5). Open 6:30 a.m. to sunset.

DESCRIPTION:

This 60-acre urban wilderness is a mecca for runners and fitness walkers. At 7:00 a.m. and 5:00 p.m. there are dozens of people doing laps around the lake—a 0.75-mile circuit. Parking at these times is next to impossible; you may have to park outside on the street. Seniors especially love Chollas, since it's a good, safe place to practice a daily exercise program. The lake is open for fishing to kids under 16. Semiannual fishing derbies are held in March and November, and there have been some record catches.

Originally built in 1900, Chollas was an active reservoir until 1952. The only city lake *not* operated by the Water Utilities Department, it's a Parks and Recreation project. Besides being a good place for large and small picnics, with the usual picnic tables, barbecues, and playgrounds, and lots of shady eucalyptus trees, Chollas offers a wealth of special activities: canoeing classes, model plane and boat clubs, and a summer day camp. Guided nature walks can be arranged by calling 265-9855.

Besides the lake circuit, there's a 0.5-mile nature trail, starting just past the covered picnic tables, to the north of the parking lot. Trail guides should be available at the trailhead, or ask at the office.

Cross the wooden bridge over a rock-lined stream—actually an irrigation ditch. There are plantings of nonnative ferns, philodendrons, and jade plants growing between the rivulets—definitely more of man than nature here.

The trail climbs gradually, curving westward. Beyond the fence, you can't miss noticing the navy's red-and-white radio towers, dwarfing everything in sight. Keep to the rock-lined path, heading back toward the water. At about #7, things start looking a little more "natural." You'll see prickly pear, buckwheat, and laurel sumac.

Circle around the wood railing or cut up the small hill, noting on your left the few scrawny chollas—"jumping cactus"—that are the lake's namesakes.

Just past Mouse Mesa is a choice of benches where you can sit unobserved and watch a birdbath where goldfinches, hummingbirds, scrub jays, and mockingbirds often drop by for a dip or a drink. The upper bench near the barrier fence gives a more unobstructed view.

Back on your feet again, you'll see a bigger patch of chollas at #15. From here, go left, along the upper side of the cactus garden, and start heading back. Just past the cactus garden is a small lushly planted section—the prettiest part of the walk. There's mint growing in the little stream, and, above the pastel lantana, a tall clump of purple-flowered marsh fleabane.

Up ahead are a few benches with tree-branch backrests, before you head down to the lake and back to the lot—unless you're ready for that 0.75-mile lap around the water.

Santee Lakes

LOCATION:

Santee. Entrance on Carlton Oaks Drive (TB47:E4). Open 8:00 a.m. to sunset. $1.00 parking fee on weekdays, $2.00 on weekends and holidays.

Feeding ducks at Lindo Lake

DESCRIPTION:

Part of a 190-acre property owned and operated by the Padre Dam Municipal Water District, this chain of seven small lakes offers fishing, boating, camping, and lots of onshore activities in a quiet suburban setting. Lakes are stocked with trout and catfish. Rowboats, pedal boats, and canoes are available for rental all summer long and on winter weekends. Volleyball and horseshoe equipment can be rented too. There are playgrounds, group picnic areas with barbecues, and a general store where you can buy fishing permits, state licenses, food, drink, and a variety of picnic and camping supplies. Lakes 6 and 7 are reserved for the exclusive use of campers; the other five lakes are open to all, and can be hiked or biked around.

To us, this park's most attractive feature is that it's all done with reclaimed sewage water—a useful and beautiful solution to our water shortage problems. Another attractive feature: handicapped access throughout the park. For information and reservations, call 448-2482.

Park in the spaces just past the entrance, to the left, beside the first lake. Here you have a chance to get up close and personal with some of Santees' coots, which are practically tame. You can look right into their beady eyes and marvel at their three-lobed chartreuse toes.

The paved 2.3-mile vehicle road around Lakes 1 through 5 doesn't need much instruction—just park and go. This is a good place for a bicycle; walkers would do well to stay on the grass, and out of the way of cars.

The main facilities are near Lake 5, at 0.8 mile. At 1 mile, turn left—only campers can continue straight ahead. Stop by Lake 6 to do some birdwatching. Coots, ducks, ring-billed gulls, cormorants, snowy egrets, and night herons like to congregate here, especially in winter on fish-stocking days. Over 175 species of waterbirds and perching birds have been recorded at Santee Lakes—you should see quite a few.

Several of the lakes have little islands, suitable for picnics. On the west side of Lake 5, you can cross an arched bridge onto an island of live oaks left over from the original streamside setting.

This far side of the lakes is less traveled and more peaceful, but you'll have to cross back between Lakes 1 and 2 to return to your car.

Lindo Lake

LOCATION:

Lakeside, entrance on Lindo Lane (TB48:F3). Open 9:00 a.m. to 5:00 p.m. weekdays, 9:30 a.m. to 7:00 p.m. weekends. 50-cent parking fee on weekdays, $1.00 on weekends. Walkers and cyclists can come in before 9:00 a.m. if they park outside.

DESCRIPTION:

Lindo means "pretty" in Spanish, and Lindo Lake, maintained by the county and run by the Lakeside Community Service Association, is a pretty place to barbecue, fly a kite, or feed the ducks. There are picnic and play areas, a ballfield, tennis courts and horseshoe pits, and, of course, the lake, which is open for fishing year-round. Pedal boats are available for summer rental. For information, call 443-3696.

Originally dedicated as a public park in 1886, when the new township of Lakeside was promoted as the Pasadena of San Diego County, Lindo Lake is one of the county's few natural freshwater lakes. The luxurious Lakeside Inn, built here in 1887, was meant to rival the Hotel del Coronado, and featured golf links, tennis courts, outdoor dining, and boating on the lake.

In 1904, the inn's new owner claimed the park and lake as part of his property, fenced it all in, and built a racetrack around the lake. Barney Oldfield, designer of the original Oldsmobile, competed here, along with other famous race car drivers.

In 1916, a group of citizens sued to get their park back. They won, and the irate owner died soon after, stipulating in his will that the inn was to be demolished.

In the 1940s, construction of the Chet Harritt Dam and Lake Jennings cut off Lindo Lake's main source of water and one good drought turned the lake into a dry hole. Since then, well water has been pumped in to maintain a reasonable level, and murky water and rapid algae growth have been persistent problems.

Today, there's a new filtration system, part of a master plan to rehabilitate the lake and create new park facilities, including a landscaped 2.5-mile trail. For now, you can circle Lake 1 ("Little Lindo") and Lake 2 ("Big Lindo")—each a 0.75-mile circuit—and walk out on the peninsula, about 0.3 mile.

All walks start from the ranger station; "Little Lindo" is the least traveled. Cross the small bridge and pick up the trail to your right, taking a left around the lake, past willows and cattails and back out to the main road again. From here you can continue on around "Big Lindo," passing closer to the street and various forms of "civilization"—a sometimes-rowdy parking lot, group picnic areas, a community center, restrooms, a ballfield, and *lots* of ducks, geese, coots, and cormorants. Back at the ranger station, take a left onto the peninsula for a visit to the old boathouse in the middle of the lake, where you can watch the ducks, the park's perimeter, and the distant mountains.

Seaside sentinel

◆ OCEAN PIERS ◆

Fishing piers aren't just for fishing—they're good for walking too. You can watch dolphins, surfers, and whales from our ocean piers, and get a gull's-eye view of the shore. If you're fond of fishing, public piers are the only place you *don't* need a license.

Oceanside Municipal Pier

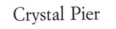

LOCATION:

Oceanside, at the end of 3rd Street. Closed during storms (TB9:C6).

DESCRIPTION:

Oceanside's first pier was a commercial wharf built in 1885, near what is now Wisconsin Street; two years later, it was a mass of rubble. Since then, several other piers were built and destroyed by storms, including the 1132-foot recreational pier built here in 1927.

Reopened in 1987, the pier is now 1942 feet long, with restrooms, a bait shop, and a restaurant at the end. Names of all local donors are engraved into the wooden railing; it's nice to see so much community support.

If you don't feel like walking, a "people mover" will taxi you from one end of the pier to the other for 25 cents—but only during restaurant hours.

Crystal Pier

LOCATION:

Pacific Beach, at the foot of Garnet Street (TB52:A4). Open 7:00 a.m. to sunset.

DESCRIPTION:

Only 720 feet long, the Crystal Pier was 1000 feet until the winter of 1982–83 when stormy seas claimed a chunk of it. The motel here is the only place in California you can sleep over the ocean. Just past the motel are bait, snack, and souvenir concessions.

The Crystal Pier opened in 1927, its main attraction a deluxe ballroom with crystal chandeliers and a cork floor to keep dancing feet from getting tired. Unfortunately, the ballroom wasn't braced properly, and all but the hardiest dancers became seasick as they whirled around the floor.

In a few months, the pilings were riddled with holes from boring marine worms; no one had thought to coat the pilings with protective creosote.

The entire pier was condemned and not reopened again until 1936; the cottages were a new addition. Over the decades, storms have subtracted one cottage and left the others somewhat the worse for wear, but the pier is still a pleasant if creaky place for a short walk and a backwards view of the busy beach scene.

A major facelift of the pier and its cottages is planned for the near future.

Ocean Beach Municipal Pier

◆

LOCATION:

Ocean Beach, at the foot of Niagara. Stair access from the parking lot at Newport. Closed during storms (TB59:A4).

DESCRIPTION:

Built in 1966, this T-shaped concrete pier extends 1971 feet into the ocean. We've seen lobster, stingrays, and halibut caught here. There's a bait shop, and a restaurant, usually with a pelican or two on the roof. From the end, you'll have a good view of surfers riding their waves into the beach.

Imperial Beach Municipal Pier

◆

LOCATION:

Imperial Beach, at Seacoast and Evergreen (TB70Z:E4). Closed during storms.

DESCRIPTION:

Built in 1909 to lure would-be home buyers from Imperial County to the beach, Imperial Beach's original pier was designed to generate electricity with the Edwards Wave Motor, which used the energy of the waves to turn generators. It was a good idea, but it didn't quite work out.

The old pier, however, survived until the winter of 1982–83, when severe storm damage shut it down. The new pier, over 1000 feet long, includes a bait shop and snack bar.

Agave

◆ SECRET GARDENS ◆

Rosicrucian Fellowship Gardens

LOCATION:

Oceanside. 2222 Mission Boulevard, at Amix Street (TB9:E4).

DESCRIPTION:

The International Headquarters of the Rosicrucians was established on this mesa top in 1911, four years after founder Max Heindel inspired the creation of the Fellowship of the Rose Cross.

Park in the guest parking area, and look for the "Meditation Walk" sign at the north side of the lot. The paved, 10-minute walk leads to the rose gardens near the 12-sided temple, whose shape represents the 12 signs of the zodiac. From there, you have a broad view of the San Luis Rey Valley below.

There's good birdwatching along the way. You should see western bluebirds and other migratory birds, especially if you come in the morning or late afternoon.

Quail Botanical Gardens

LOCATION:

Encinitas, on Quail Gardens Drive, north of Encinitas Boulevard (TB24:E4). Open 8:00 a.m. to 5:00 p.m. in winter, 8:00 a.m. to 6:00 p.m. in summer. $1.00 parking fee.

DESCRIPTION:

This pleasant county park features 30 acres of palms, ferns, hibiscus, bamboo, and hundreds of other exotic plants from all over the world. There are natives too, but the exotics here are much more interesting. Come on a weekday morning, when there's no one else around, and you're likely to see a family of quail skittering across the path; after all, this is Quail Gardens.

Even if you don't see quail, you should hear them. Listen for the call "Cuidado! Cuidado!," which means "Be careful" in Spanish. Once this sentry call is sounded, the rest of the covey clicks softly to each other, making sure everyone gets the message.

At the visitor's center, there's a small gift shop with a nice collection of books and nature knicknacks, open 11:00 a.m. to 3:00 p.m., Wednesday, Friday, Saturday, and Sunday. Outside, check the "What's Happening" board for lectures, concerts, plant sales, and other events, and pick up a brochure and map. Free docent-led tours start here every Saturday at 10:00 a.m., weather permitting.

Don't miss the Mildred MacPherson Waterfall, framed by tropical foliage—a peaceful place to dream away a few moments. Follow the falls down to a water lily pond, where you'll often see the resident turtle sunning himself or swimming through the murky water. There are koi here too, those colorful Japanese carp that can live as long as a human and cost as much as a house.

In spring, the pondside jacaranda trees are covered with purple blossoms. When the blossoms fall, you can see flowering bromeliads, called "air plants," growing in the jacaranda branches.

Make your way downhill to Palm Canyon, where, in summer, you'll see orange dates in the tall palms and on the ground; they look more like apricots than the brown oval fruits we're used to.

In the South African section, along the service road, there's a pink-flowered virgilia that local birds really love. On our last trip, we saw Allen's hummingbirds courting here, the male doing a series of dramatic swoops to impress the female. There were at least a dozen or more bushtits and goldfinches in the branches, searching for edible insects.

Nearby are the proteas, those unbeautiful, oddly endearing flowers that look like artichokes, corncobs, oversized bottle-brushes—anything but flowers.

On a recent visit, we had a thrilling bit of good luck. Just behind the visitor's center, as we were leaving, we saw a gray fox, probably on its way to sample some of the fallen dates in Palm Canyon. Here's wishing you the same happy serendipity!

Self Realization Fellowship Meditation Gardens

◆

LOCATION:

Encinitas, 215 K Street. Look for the gilded lotus domes of the S.R.F. on Highway 101 (TB24:D5). Open 9:00 a.m. to 5:00 p.m., Tuesday through Saturday, 11:00 a.m. to 5:00 p.m. Sunday.

DESCRIPTION:

A quiet spot, beautifully landscaped, with an unbeatable view of the sea, this is a fine place for watching surfers, dolphins, whales, and early sunsets. Off-limits to the public is the hermitage built for Swami Yogananda (1893–1952), founder of the S.R.F., who loved to meditate here. Local legend has it that this spot was once a power place for California Indians, long before the swamis discovered America.

Flowering plants are changed regularly, so the garden looks a bit different every time you visit. The mini-walk leads past two small koi ponds, which, in 1988, were covered over with netting after some of the local herons figured out this was a great place for a free lunch. Strategically placed stone benches are often occupied by meditators, but you can usually stake one out for yourself. The beach below is called, not unnaturally, Swami's, and has some of our favorite tidepools (see Swami's Park, p. 191).

Great egrets

WILD WINGS:
◆ A BIRDWATCHER'S GUIDE ◆

Like walking, birding is one of the most popular outdoor activities in the U.S. today. San Diego offers great birdwatching, with over 450 species of birds to be found throughout the county. Any one of our walks can be turned into a bird walk with the proper equipment—a pair of binoculars and a field guide. Here are a few good places for beginners to try.

Libby Lake

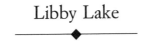

LOCATION:

Oceanside. Access on Calle Montecito from North River Road (TB7:C6).

DESCRIPTION:

A small freshwater pond. Look for ducks, coots, grebes, and moorhens in the water. Look for shrikes, goldfinches, and hawks in the chaparral.

Buena Vista Lagoon

LOCATION:

Carlsbad. Access on frontage road from Jefferson, just south of Highway 78 (TB13:F2, E3).

DESCRIPTION:

Open water viewing of ducks, cormorants, and terns. There's a new Audubon Nature Center on Hill Street, open 10:00 a.m. to 2:00 p.m., Tuesday through Saturday, with exhibits of local birds and wildlife. Walk out on the narrow fishermen's paths to see more secretive birds like Virginia rails, soras, and moorhens.

Batiquitos Lagoon

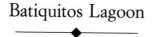

LOCATION:

Carlsbad. Access on Batiquitos Drive from Poinsettia (TB19:D5).

DESCRIPTION:

Major development is changing the upland area here, and dredging will change the lagoon itself. Along the north shore, look for ducks, grebes, phalaropes, Bonaparte's gulls, and terns.

San Dieguito Reservoir

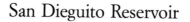

LOCATION:

Rancho Santa Fe. Access at San Elijo and El Montevideo (TB26:A6).

DESCRIPTION:

Follow the path outside the fence to see cormorants, Canada geese, western grebes, and diving ducks.

San Dieguito Lagoon

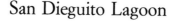

LOCATION:

Del Mar. Access at San Dieguito Drive and Grand Avenue (TB34:A1).

DESCRIPTION:

In this restored wetland, on the site of the old Del Mar Airport, look for osprey, kingfishers, terns, ducks, and many kinds of shorebirds.

San Diego Flood Control Channel

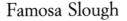

LOCATION:

San Diego. Access from Sea World Drive between Sea World Way and Friars Road (TB59:D2).

DESCRIPTION:

From the frontage road, you can see ducks, egrets, herons, and shorebirds. Sometimes there are burrowing owls in the rocks and peregrine falcons flying overhead.

Famosa Slough

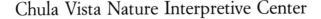

LOCATION:

Loma Portal. Access at West Point Loma Boulevard and Famosa Boulevard (TB59:C3).

DESCRIPTION:

This remnant of old False Bay (now Mission Bay) is great for beginners, because you can see birds up close. Blue-winged teal come here every winter, and many kinds of ducks and shorebirds are usually in residence.

Chula Vista Nature Interpretive Center

LOCATION:

Chula Vista. Park at the foot of E Street, just off I-5 (TB69:B4). A shuttle bus (50 cents round trip) leaves every 20 minutes from 10:00 a.m. to 4:30 p.m.

DESCRIPTION:

A living wetlands museum, the only one of its kind in Southern California. From its observation platforms, you can see some of the 130 bird species that visit surrounding Sweetwater Marsh. Look for hawks, egrets, and the uncommon little blue heron. For guided birdwalks, call 422-BIRD. Closed Mondays.

Outside the Chula Vista Nature Interpretive Center. Photo by Barbara Moore

South Bay Biological Study Area

◆

LOCATION:

Coronado near Imperial Beach. Access from Highway 75, "The Silver Strand" (TB70Z:F2).

DESCRIPTION:

These 27 acres of county-owned wetlands are home to many marsh-loving birds. At low tide, stroll out on the dikes jutting into the bay to see shorebirds, diving ducks, black skimmers, and sea geese.

APPENDICES

A: NATIVE PLANTS OF THE CHAPARRAL

B: IMAGES OF NATURE

C: SUGGESTED READING

Appendix A
Native Plants of the Chaparral

◆

Drawings by Kathryn Watson

For easy reference, we've listed all entries alphabetically by common name. Latin names are included for more precise identification.

BROOM (*Baccharis sarothroides*)

Indians made brooms, brushes, and even toothbrushes out of this rough-textured shrub, which has short narrow leaves and cottony, cream-colored flowers. No relation to Scotch broom, chaparral broom usually indicates an area of *disturbed chaparral,* where the land was once cleared for farming or grazing cattle.

BUCKWHEAT (*Eriogonum fasciculatum*)

Once you learn to recognize its reddish-brown seed clusters, you'll see buckwheat everywhere. In spring, it's covered with pink buds and white flowers. This isn't the buckwheat that pancakes are made from, but Indians did grind the seeds into cakes and mush. A strong tea brewed from the leaves was said to cure headaches and stomach aches. Used as a mouthwash, it strengthened gums and teeth. Blossoms were steeped into a soothing eye wash.

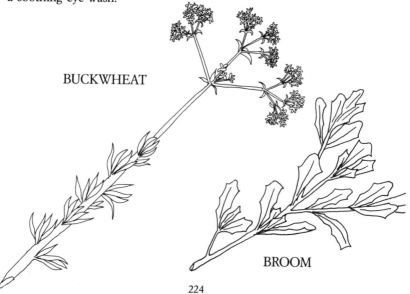

BUCKWHEAT

BROOM

PRICKLY PEAR

BARREL CACTUS

CHOLLA

CACTI

BARREL CACTUS (*Ferocactus viridescens*). Round and squat, this small cactus often grows in open areas and has yellow flowers in spring. Indians used its spines for tattoo needles.

CHOLLA (*Opuntia prolifera*). The slim-branched cholla is commonly called "jumping cactus" because its joints break off easily and stick to clothes and skin. Spring flowers may be yellow or red.

PRICKLY PEAR (*Opuntia littoralis*). The spiny flat pads of the prickly pear cactus sprout pink buds in winter, yellow flowers in spring, and red fruit in fall. The fruit is rough and prickly on the outside, but sweet inside. Watch out for the prickles; you can get a mouthful if you're not *very* careful (we speak from experience).

A cultivated variety of this cactus is cooked and served as *nopales* in Mexican restaurants. The fruits, called *tunas,* are the basis of several Mexican sweets.

In summer, prickly pear pads are covered with powdery white patches of cochineal, scale insects related to mealybugs. Female insects were collected, dried, and ground into a brilliant red dye, which, next to gold, was the most prized export from New Spain. It was used to color royal robes, tapestries, religious vestments, and the red coats of the British army.

CEANOTHUS (*Ceanothus,* various species)

Ranging in color from white to lavender blue, ceanothus, or wild lilac, has something of the look of miniature lilacs, but none of the fragrance. The common coastal variety is sometimes called popcorn bush because of the popping sound made when the seed pods burst open in summer and shoot seeds all over the ground. Indians ground the seeds into flour for mush and made mush stirrers from the wood. A wash from the leaves was used to relieve itching, especially from poison oak.

CHAMISE (*Adenostoma fasciculatum*)

Nicknamed greasewood, chamise is tough on firefighters, since, like grease, it burns fast and furiously, and gives off a thick black smoke. Its name comes from the Spanish *chamiso,* a kind of crude brushwood shack that can catch fire easily. Indians used the wood for arrow shafts and throwing sticks. Tea made from the tiny needle-like leaves was said to cure tetanus, rabies, and syphilis.

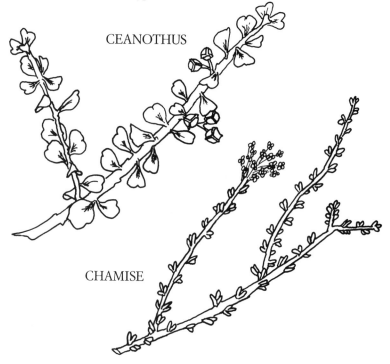

CEANOTHUS

CHAMISE

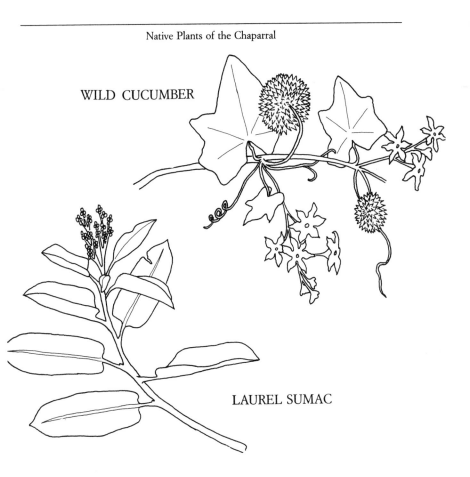

WILD CUCUMBER

LAUREL SUMAC

CUCUMBER, WILD (*Marah macrocarpus*)

Called "manroot" by the Indians, wild cucumber indeed has a man-sized root that is very difficult to dig up if you want to remove it from your property. Cucumber vines have a way of getting their curly tendrils around everything that grows in their vicinity. The prickly fruits are inedible, but Indians ate the seeds and used their oil as a cure for baldness. Pulverized roots were thrown into the water to stun fish and bring them to the surface for easy netting.

LAUREL SUMAC (*Rhus laurina*)

Since it's supposed to live only in frost-free areas, growers look for laurel sumac to determine where to plant citrus trees and avocados. The large leaves resemble bay laurel; on hot days those leaves exposed to the sun fold up to conserve water.

LEMONADE BERRY (*Rhus integrifolia*)

Lemonade berry belongs to the same family as laurel sumac and poison oak. The clusters of small pinkish "berries" you see in winter are really flowers; the sticky red fruit doesn't form until spring. A few berries dropped in a canteen can turn plain water into a lemony drink.

MANZANITA (*Arctostaphylos,* various species)

Manzanita means "little apple" in Spanish, and manzanita berries do look like tiny apples. Indians ate the fruit; pioneers turned it into cider. Some tribes made a wash from the leaves to soothe the itching of poison oak. The smooth reddish wood was carved into spoons and pipes, and its twisted burls were so prized by tourists and decorators that manzanita was in danger of extinction. Today, all species of manzanita are protected by California law.

MONKEY FLOWER, BUSH (*Mimulus puniceus*)

These pretty trumpet-shaped red or orange flowers may bloom anytime, but especially in the spring. Tea was brewed from the flowers, leaves, and stems to combat "Montezuma's revenge"—diarrhea.

POISON OAK (*Rhus diversiloba*)

"Leaves of three, let it be." Poison oak's three-leaf clusters are shiny green in the spring and bright red in the fall, but even in winter, with no leaves at all, it still means trouble, and touching the naked stems can give you a painful, itchy, blistering rash.

Urushiol, the oil produced by the plant, is so toxic that even inhaling the smoke from a brush fire can be dangerous. Petting an animal that has run through a patch of poison oak can be a problem too, though animals themselves don't seem to be affected, and many birds eat the berries and spread the seeds.

Certain Indian tribes managed to get along with poison oak by taking small doses of it to immunize themselves; some baked bread wrapped in its leaves and others applied the leaves to rattlesnake bites. If you think you've come in contact with it, wash the area as soon as possible with soap and water, and hope for the best.

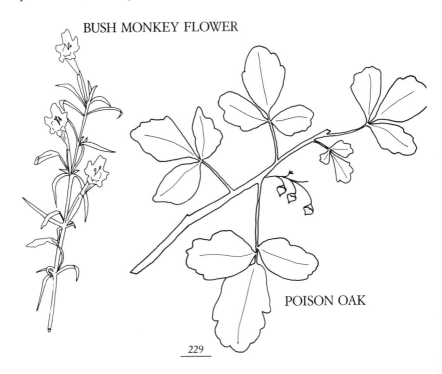

BUSH MONKEY FLOWER

POISON OAK

BLACK SAGE

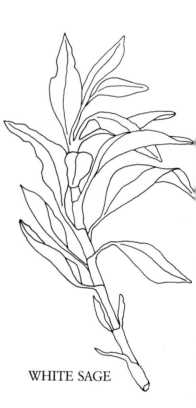

WHITE SAGE

SAGE (*Salvia,* various species)

If you smell something that reminds you of Thanksgiving, you're probably not far from a sage plant. Members of the mint family, all sages are related to the herb that flavors turkey stuffing.

BLACK SAGE (*Salvia mellifera*) with its dark green leaves and lavender blue flowers is generally found along the coast. The tips can be added to salads, and the leaves can be used in cooking.

WHITE SAGE (*S. apiana*), more common in inland areas, has large, soft, grayish leaves with small orchidlike white flowers that bees love. Indians ate the seeds, and made a tea from the leaves to treat colds and serious cases of poison oak. White sage was used in purification rituals, and also as a natural deodorant—men slept with it before a hunt to cover their human scent.

SAGEBRUSH (*Artemesia californica*)

Sagebrush, with its soft, feathery, gray-green leaves, is no relation to sage, although it does smell somewhat sagey. It's related to tarragon, absinthe, and other members of the sunflower family. Indians brewed sagebrush tea to induce menstruation and to ensure an easy childbirth and quick recovery. They also taught early settlers its usefulness as a flea repellant.

SCRUB OAK (*Quercus dumosa*)

This evergreen shrub called *chaparro,* or "shorty," by Mexican cowboys is what gives the chaparral its name. Each plant has slightly different leaves and acorns. Birds and animals seem to like the acorns well enough, but Indians ate them only in emergencies. They preferred the bigger, sweeter acorns of the coast live oak as a staple food, and made annual treks to the mountains to gather black oak acorns, their favorite of all.

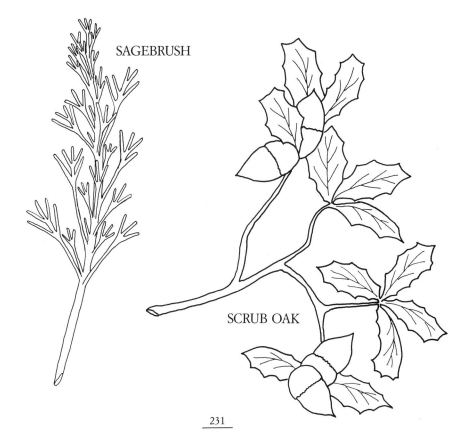

SAGEBRUSH

SCRUB OAK

TOYON (*Heteromeles arbutifolia*)

Sometimes called Christmas berry or California holly, toyon can be recognized by its jagged leaves and bright red berries, which may appear as early as Halloween. Hollywood was named for this tall bush, which, years ago, covered its hills. Summer flowers are white, small, and unremarkable. The berries, a favorite food of birds, foxes, and other wildlife, were cooked and eaten by Indians, who also brewed a tea from the bark and leaves to use as a painkiller.

YUCCAS

MOJAVE YUCCA (*Yucca schidigera*), or Spanish bayonet, is most common along the coast. From the center of its broad, pointed leaves, it sends up stalks that look like giant asparagus. Within weeks, they are topped with long clusters of cream-colored flowers. Indians used the tough, stringy fibers curling out of the leaves to make rope, thread, horse blankets, sandals, and baskets.

WHIPPLE'S YUCCA (*Yucca whipplei*), sometimes called Our Lord's Candle, has narrower leaves, an even taller flower stalk, and finer thread-making fibers, which, during World War I, were used to make burlap. It blooms only once and then dies, while Spanish bayonet blooms year after year. Buds and seed pods were toasted and eaten by Indians.

At night, flowering yuccas seem to glow in the moonlight and smell almost as sweet as night-blooming jasmine. This attracts the night-flying yucca moths that lay eggs in the flowers, and pollinate them. Each species of yucca has its own exclusive pollinator; it's a symbiotic relationship, with plant and moth dependent on each other for survival.

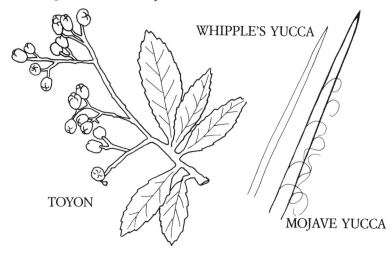

WHIPPLE'S YUCCA

TOYON

MOJAVE YUCCA

Appendix B: Images of Nature

◆

Many people enjoy creating their own souvenirs of the "wild." Here are three suggestions that are inexpensive, easy, and fun to do.

LEAF RUBBINGS

What You Need

Clipboard
Paper
Charcoal pencil or crayon
Leaf

What To Do

Find a leaf with interesting ridges, veins, texture, or shape. Clip the leaf by its stem to the clipboard, with its rough surface up. Place paper on top. Using the side of your charcoal pencil or crayon, color across the entire surface of the leaf. An image of the leaf will appear.

Experiment with different strokes and pressures to get the results you like best. When finished, you may want to outline the edge or cut out the rubbing and mount it on a paper of contrasting color.

PRESSING SEAWEEDS

What You Need

2 cake cooling racks
Corrugated cardboard, cut to the same size as the cake racks
Paper (index cards, typing, botany, or watercolor paper)
Paper towels
2 elastic bike cords
1 shallow pan
Water
Assorted seaweeds

What To Do

1. Wash each seaweed specimen well to remove sand.
2. Arrange each one carefully on your choice of paper.
3. Start layering in this order:
   a. cake rack
   b. cardboard
   c. paper towels (several)

d. 1st seaweed
e. paper towels
f. cardboard
g. paper towels
h. 2nd seaweed
i. paper towels
j. and so on until you finish with cardboard and a cake rack on the outside

4. Tie together tightly with elastic bike cords.
5. Place the bundle outdoors in the sun, or in a warm spot like a water heater closet. Wait a week or more before opening.
6. Open carefully; if some seaweeds do not stick, a small dab of white glue will help.
7. Frame the result, or cover with clear contact paper.

MAKING TRACKS

What You Need

Plaster of Paris (available in 1-pound boxes at variety drug stores)
Container of water
½-gallon milk carton
Wooden spoon
Scissors
Several plastic shopping bags for trash

What To Do

1. Cut off the top of the milk carton—all you need is two or three 1-inch sections for mold forms. Use the rest of the carton to mix the plaster.
2. Find interesting tracks of a bird, raccoon, or coyote.
3. Place mold form around the track.
4. Mix plaster and water together to the consistency of thick pancake batter.
5. Pour plaster onto tracks and leave in the mold to harden.

Hint: You have to work quickly, and you need a clean mixing container each time you make the plaster.

Appendix C: Suggested Reading

◆

Here are some books we've particularly enjoyed. If you can't find them in your local bookstore, try museum bookshops or the public library.

GEOLOGY

Abbott, Patrick and Victoria, Janice K. *Geologic Hazards in San Diego.* San Diego: San Diego Museum of Natural History, 1977.

Kern, Phillip. *Earthquakes and Faults in San Diego.* San Diego: Pickle Press, 1983.

Kuhn, Gerald and Shepard, Francis. *Sea Cliffs, Beaches, and Coastal Valleys of San Diego.* Berkeley: University of California Press, 1984.

Moore, Ellen. *Fossil Mollusks of San Diego County.* San Diego: San Diego Museum of Natural History, 1968.

HISTORY

Almstedt, Ruth. *Diegueño Curing Practices.* San Diego: San Diego Museum Papers, 1977.

Carrico, Richard L. *Strangers in a Stolen Land.* San Diego: San Diego State University, Publications in American Indian Studies No. 2, 1986.

Fuller, Theodore W. *San Diego Originals.* Pleasant Hill: California Profiles Publications, 1987.

Hedges, Ken and Beresford, Christina. *Santa Ysabel Ethnobotany.* San Diego: San Diego Museum of Man, Ethnic Technology Notes No. 20, 1986.

Lee, Melicent. *Indians of the Oaks.* San Diego: San Diego Museum of Man, 1978.

Lockwood, Herbert. *Skeleton's Closet, Vols.* I and II. La Mesa: Bailey and Associates. (no date)

McKeever, Michael. *A Short History of San Diego.* San Francisco: Lexicos, 1985.

Mills, James R. *San Diego, Where California Began.* San Diego: San Diego Historical Society, 1985.

Pourade, Richard, ed. *Historic Ranchos of San Diego.* San Diego: Union Tribune Publishing Company, 1969.

————, ed. *The History of San Diego,* 7 vols. San Diego: Union Tribune Publishing Company, 1960–1977.

Shipek, Florence. *The Autobiography of Delfina Cuero.* Morongo Indian Reservation: Malki Museum Press, 1970.

Stein, Lou. *San Diego County Place Names.* San Diego: Rand Editions, Tofua Press, 1975.

Ward, Mary. *Rancho de Los Peñasquitos, On the Road to Yuma.* San Diego: County of San Diego, Department of Parks and Recreation, 1984.

NATURAL HISTORY

Balls, Edward K. *Early Uses of California Plants.* Berkeley: University of California Press, 1962.

Belzer, Thomas. *Roadside Plants of Southern California.* Missoula: Mountain Press Publishing Co., 1984.

Berger, Wolf. *Walk Along the Ocean.* Alhambra: Border Mountain Press, 1976.

Clarke, Charlotte B. *Edible and Useful Plants of California.* Berkeley: University of California Press, 1977.

Dale, Nancy. *Flowering Plants of the Santa Monica Mountains, Coastal and Chaparral Regions of Southern California.* Santa Barbara: Capra Press, 1986.

Head, W. S. *The California Chaparral: An Elfin Forest.* Healdsburg: Naturegraph Publishers, 1972.

Hinton, Sam. *Seashore Life of Southern California.* Berkeley: University of California Press, 1987.

Meyer, Ruth S. *Some Highlights of the Natural History of San Diego County.* Ramona: Ramona Pioneer Historical Society, 1981.

Nicol, Hank. *Notes from the Naturalist.* Del Mar: Torrey Pines Docent Society, 1981.

Witham, Helen. *Ferns of San Diego County.* San Diego: San Diego Museum of Natural History, 1972.

GENERAL

California Coastal Commission. *California Coastal Resource Guide.* Berkeley: University of California Press, 1987.

Ebner, Rose Boehm. *San Diego Companion.* San Diego: Self-published, 1987.

McWilliams, Carey. *Southern California, an Island On the Land.* Salt Lake City: Peregrine Smith edition, 1988.

Pryde, Philip, ed. *San Diego: An Introduction to the Region.* Dubuque: Kendall Hunt Publishing Co., 1984.

SAN DIEGO GUIDE BOOKS

Mendel, Carol. *San Diego on Foot.* San Diego: Self-published, 1975.

———— *San Diego... City & County.* San Diego: Self-published, 6th ed., 1987.

Schad, Jerry. *Afoot and Afield in San Diego County.* Berkeley: Wilderness Press, 1986.

Tucker, Joan. *San Diego and the Southland—Just the Facts.* Leucadia: Rand Editions, 1984.

◆INDEX◆

City names appear in boldface; illustrations in italic.

About the Authors:

LONNIE BURSTEIN HEWITT is a writer, whose credits range from Broadway musicals to *Sesame Street.* Her articles on outdoor activities have appeared in a number of San Diego area newspapers, and she is a regular contributor to the *San Diego Tribune.*

BARBARA COFFIN MOORE is a naturalist, who has been leading walks through San Diego's chaparral, wetlands, beaches, and hillsides for over 15 years. She trains docents at Scripps Aquarium, and frequently writes on topics of natural history.

Both women are longtime residents of San Diego County.